Becoming Brands: Celebrity, Activism and Politics

Edited by

Jackie Raphael and Celia Lam

WH

WATERHILL
PUBLISHING

ISBN 978-0-9939938-8-6

The views and opinions expressed herein are those of the authors and do not necessarily reflect the positions of the publisher.

Contents

List of Contributors

Dr. Alexander Araya López grew up in San José, Costa Rica. He studied Sociology at the Universidad de Costa Rica and finished his PhD studies at the Lateinamerika Institut, Freie Universität Berlin in 2014. His research is focused on media studies with an emphasis on crime, security and public spaces.

Dr. Evan Beaumont Center researches Popular Culture and Social Justice. He teaches Media Studies & Rhetoric at Christopher Newport University and holds a PhD in Communication from the University of Kansas.

Marie Josephine Bennett is a PhD student at the University of Winchester, where she is examining representations of LGBTQ characters in film musicals post Stonewall. Publications include chapters in *Protest Music in the Twentieth Century* (2016) and *Cinema Invites Other Gazes* (2016), and an article in *The Soundtrack* journal (2014).

Ellen Finlay is a current Masters of International Relations (IR) student at the University of Sydney having completed her undergraduate degree in Politics and Sociology with first class Honours in IR at the University of Notre Dame Australia.

Kelly M. O'Donnell is a second-year M.A. student at UNC- Greensboro. Her research focuses on rhetoric in online communication, feminist rhetorical criticism, and critical activism pedagogy. Her work can be found in the *Working Papers in Education* online journal and a co-authored chapter in *Truth in the Public Sphere*.

Dr. Tomasz Olczyk is assistant professor at University of Warsaw (Applied Social Sciences Institute). He holds a PhD in sociology, and his work focuses on intersections between popular culture and politics. His main research interests include televised political advertising and celebrity politics.

Dr. Jackie Raphael teaches at Curtin University and focuses her research on endorsements and bromances. She is on the Advisory Board of CMCS and the *Celebrity Chat* producer. She has published various papers and has co-edited books such as *Credibility and the Incredible: Disassembling the Celebrity Figure* and *Bridging Gaps in Celebrity Studies.*

Carla Rocavert holds a Bachelor of Arts (Communication - Theatre / Media) and a Master of Arts (Cultural Event Management) from Charles Sturt University. Before joining the University of Tasmania she worked at Australian theatre and film festivals and in artist management. Her research investigates the ways reality entertainment displaces creativity.

Dr. Louise St Guillaume currently works as a Lecturer in Sociology and Social Justice in the School of Arts and Sciences, UNDA. Louise is the 2011 winner of the Australian Critical Race and Whiteness Studies e-journal essay competition (non-Indigenous submission). Her current research interests include disability, welfare, migration and Indigenous policy in Australia and celebrity advocacy, disability and human rights.

Dr. Ronald Strickland is a Professor of Literature and Chair of the Humanities Department at Michigan Technological University. He is the editor of *Growing Up postmodern: Neoliberalism and the war on the young*, and a special edition of the journal *Humanities*: "Saving the Humanities from the neoliberal university."

Dr. Sally Totman is Associate Professor of Middle East Studies at Deakin University. She is the author of *How Hollywood Projects Foreign Policy* (Palgrave Macmillan, 2009) as well as numerous articles on Middle East politics and international relations.

Dr. Nilay Ulusoy is an Associate Professor at Bahcesehir University. She received her PhD degree from Marmara University for her dissertation on "Political Economy of Turkish Cinema". She teaches courses on the film history, film theory. Her fields of interest include language of fashion and Turkish cinema in the 2000s.

Dr. Jacek Wasilewski was awarded a PhD with a dissertation on Polish identity narratives. He is the founder of the Document Studies at the University of Warsaw. He is a semiotician, expert in communication and avid follower of popular culture. He is interested in the intricacies of meaning. He is a storytelling expert in advertising.

Foreword:
The Bridge of the Human Brand

P. David Marshall

It seems brands and branding in contemporary culture has become both ubiquitous and accepted. The pervasiveness of brands identifies their relation to the way that corporations identify their value. One of the most interesting phenomenon of the twentieth century is how corporate accounting practices changed in the 1980s to calibrate brand value as an asset – and clearly, in many corporations, the brand is its most valuable asset (Moor, 2007).

Understanding branding just from this economic dimension does not capture the full impact of brands however. It is easy to forget how at least historically branding was a quite physical transformation of animals and humans to proclaim ownership: the branding of cattle to claim the livestock as property continues as a phenomenon, while the branding of humans as property and slaves is generally seen as something that is well beyond the acceptable.

So, it comes as an interesting development in the history of branding that it now is often very much a valued and permissible status to transform an individual into a brand. Our most visible human brands are of course celebrities and they collectively identify, when they are branded, a way in which a human is converted into an economic value; a commodity that may have transformative value for other products and services. As Jackie Raphael's chapter in this book identifies through Grant McCracken's foundational work, the celebrity's brand is a form of transference. Celebrities possess emotional connections to their audiences, which is convertible into an affective connection to the associated product that they endorse or embrace in some way. Celebrities as brands can be used to sell forms of entertainment – that is, the star of a film is designed to draw a new audience often based on their past acting work to the new cultural product. But celebrities are also used with regularity in other domains as 'brand' ambassadors or endorsers. Sports stars are 'sponsored' by the companies who produce the products they wear. Online micro-celebrities for instance in fashion or cosmetics similarly establish an affirming relationship with products that aligns these products with what these individuals see as valuable for their audiences.

In a more complex way, the branded celebrity is also used in philanthropic and political causes. As several chapters explore in this book, the celebrity is a key figure in the contemporary attention economy in their capacity to bring the world's attention to particular causes, struggles and issues. But human brands such as celebrities are never just branded products. They contain within them some competing forms of value, compromising ethics, and perhaps elaborate back and future-stories that make their attachment to issues variegated to say the least.

It is easy to dismiss this pervasive human branding as a negative phenomenon. After all, it appears to be a reduction/conversion of the human spirit and ethos into a commodity for transfer and exchange with other commodities and products. However, as this book explores, the development of the human brand and its pervasiveness as an accepted way of presenting an individual in the contemporary moment contains within it a certain pragmatism and strategizing by both the individuals involved, and the institutions that link themselves to these constructed attention-grabbing identities.

Two further elements complicate the now standard neo-liberal critique of this form of public individuality. The first is that the 'human brand' is not a new phenomenon. It has circulated around and through what could be described as democratic capitalism for the last two centuries. Tom Mole, for instance, described the way in which Lord Byron negotiated his public presence in the world like a brand in the early nineteenth century, although the terminology was certainly not standard at the time (2007). In a recent update of his work, Loren Glass similarly links Mark Twain's late 19th and twentieth century work with branding his identity for greater reach and impact (2016).

Brand culture has similarly invaded our political discourse as we rethink politicians and parties as 'political' brands which have worked to navigate through the attention economy in a manner similar to commercial products, and different patterns of entertainment culture, for as much as 100 years (see Speed, Butler & Collins, 2015; and Marshall & Henderson, 2016). The pop star, the movie star and the current YouTube star are all branded entities used to promote cultural commodities through the now complex attention economy.

From this apparent expansion and standardization of branding into a modern public identity designed for specific – and usually economic – purposes, the second element that complicates the neo-liberal critique of branding emerges. My own recent work has identified that twinned with the expansion of online culture and its generation of social media, as platforms of activity, is the pervasive proliferation of billions of individuals constructing public identities or 'personas' (see for instance Marshall, 2016a). Personas are strategic identities that are used to navigate a public world. Although personas are not identical to a branded identity, they are nonetheless the pathway for individuals to move with relative ease into imagining their public profiles as feeding into a commodified self.

The human brand has become a bridge for the movement of ideas, the realignment and refocus on issues in cultures, the expression of goodwill and assistance, and, of course - its bedrock - the movement of commodities. The human brand, along with branding more generally, identifies a formation of agency that I have called "industrialized agency" because of its link to this commodity structure and its further alignment with the reconfiguration of the individual into a strategic public entity and identity that can be used – and deployed by others – for particular goals and outcomes (Marshall, 2016b).

This book provides an elaborate and valued study of how the human brand operates as a bridge in contemporary culture. The complexity of meanings that are part of the human brand ensure that one of its primary purposes is to express emotion and congeal that emotion into a human face and identity. In this book, there is a close study of activism and the way in which celebrities provide the bridge to identify the significance of given issues. Human brands sometimes make complex issues personalized and perhaps through that channel, understandable.

In the four sections of this book, there is an exploration of the different kinds of bridges that the famed have made in our culture. From an investigation of the contradictions and successes of activism and direct implications into political culture, to working out the place and agency of feminism and philanthropic value, the contributors weave a tapestry of sometimes conflicted engagement. The very successful people discussed in this book have used their 'brands' and translated them into different settings with quite different objectives. All of the analyses give us an entrée into the current mechanisms of this human brand bridge and provide insights into this now normalized dimension of our pandemic persona culture: industrialized agency.

References

Glass, L. (2016). Brand Names: A Brief History of Literary Celebrity. In P. D. Marshall & S. Redmond (Eds.), *A Companion to Celebrity* (pp. 39-57). Boston: Blackwell-Wiley.

Marshall, P. D. (2016a). *The Celebrity Persona Pandemic* (Forerunner series). Minneapolis: University of Minnesota Press.

Marshall, P. D. (2016b, July). *Commodifying the Celebrity-Self: The Peculiar Emergence, Formation and Value of "Industrial" Agency in the Contemporary Attention Economy*. Keynote Presentation at the Bridging Gaps: What are the media, publicists and celebrities selling? Conference. Barcelona, Spain: Centre for Media and Celebrity Studies.

Marshall, P. D. (2017). Commodifying the Celebrity Self: The Peculiar Emergence, Formation and Value of 'Industrialized' Agency in the Contemporary Attention Economy. *Zeitschrift für Medienwissenschaft (ZfM)*. 16 (April).

Marshall, P. D. & Henderson, N. (2016). Political Persona 2016 – An Introduction. *Persona Studies.* 2 (2), 1-18. Retrieved from https://ojs.deakin.edu.au/index.php/ps/issue/view/98/showToc.

Mole, T. (2007). *Byron's Romantic Celebrity: Industrial Culture and the Hermeneutic of Intimacy.* New York: Palgrave Macmillan.

Moor, L. (2007). *The Rise of Brands.* Oxford and New York: Berg.

Speed, R., Patrick, B., & Collins, N. (2015). Human Branding in Political Marketing: Applying Contemporary Branding Thought to Political Parties and Their Leaders. *Journal of Political Marketing,* 14(1.2), 129-151.

Introduction: Becoming Brands

Jackie Raphael and Celia Lam

Bridging Brands

Popular culture plays a pivotal role in the world, creating political, social and economic influences. The advertising industry relies heavily on celebrities for endorsements, while more and more celebrities are becoming involved with charities to benefit both their own celebrity persona and for altruistic purposes. This means that celebrity and charity brands are often reliant on each other, and the two must be bridged to successfully communicate to audiences. A celebrity's persona becomes their brand and this is sold to fans globally. They then gain the power to inspire change yet, not all use this influence in the same way.

This book discusses the varying levels of success of celebrities who are activists or philanthropists, as well as those who have gained fame for their activism. Part one explores celebrities' various approaches to activism and levels of commitment; part two examines the importance of presentation and fame in politics; part three investigates the way female celebrities enact issues relating to feminism both on- and off-screen; and part four celebrates the impact that iconic dead celebrities have left on the world from philanthropic organizations to awareness of HIV/AIDS. Overall, this book creates a broad discussion on the power of celebrities and how their individual brands can create global change.

Bridging Ideas

Approaches to Activism

The association between activism and celebrity often occurs in public view through the scrutiny of the media. Indeed, celebrities encourage media interest if it draws attention to their causes and publicizes issues. However, the publicity associated with celebrity involvement in activism can also function as a double-edged sword, working to subsume the cause into the celebrity's broader public persona rather than focusing attention on the issue. The four chapters in this section offer an exploration of the phenomenon of celebrity activism from a variety of perspectives. Firstly, Carla Rocavert interrogates the level of celebrity commitment to activism through the lens of their on-and-off stage activity. Arguing that some celebrity activism is an extension of the performance of their on-stage public persona, Rocavert examines several celebrity case studies, and questions the ability for activism to enter the offstage space. This discussion is continued in Sally Totman's chapter, in which she explores Angelina Jolie and George Clooney's 'Super Celebrity Activist' status. In this instance their offstage activity cements their commitment as activists. Next, Ellen Finlay and Louise St Guillaume offer a critical perspective on celebrity and activism. They explore Taylor Swift's meet-and-greet sessions with fans with disability. While these sessions generate publicity for Swift and enable the creation of a positive celebrity image, Finlay and St Guillaume argue they serve to reinforce hegemonic attitudes towards disability. They thus challenge the ability of such celebrity interaction to affect change. Finally, Evan Beaumont Center explores how environmental activist, Paul Watson, has commercialised his activism in order to gain celebrity status.

Politics and Presentation

From celebrity endorsement to celebrity-turned-politicians, the contemporary political sphere seems to be inextricably linked to the sphere of celebrity. Particularly, in a media environment when celebrity is often attributed as much as they are ascribed or achieved (Rojek, 2001), public visibility can be a path to (both desired and undesired) celebrity. For some activists, celebrity can be a hindrance, as is the case of the pixadores examined by Alexander Araya López. Contrary to Brazillian graffiti artists, this group has become famous due to their 'subversive' graffiti activity, and are reluctant to adopt the celebrity that accompanies such fame, as it compromises their political integrity. Ronald Strickland's chapter bridges the world of celebrities and politicians through his exploration of the contextual meanings influencing Clint Eastwood's 'failed' speech at the 2012 Republican campaign. He connects Eastwood's identity politics to the broader historical-political context behind his films, and draws a comparison to Donald Trump's campaign four years later. Finally, Tomasz Olczyk and Jacek Wasilewski explore the persona of rock star-turned-politician Paweł Kukiz, for whom political success hinges on his celebrity persona. As a celebrity, he is a political outsider and a rebel. In order to gain political success, he has to regain this 'rebel' identity through a reconnection with his celebrity.

Facing Feminism

The two chapters in this section offer a dialogue on the role of individual celebrities in political movements, in this instance Feminist movements. Nilay Ulusoy's chapter focuses attention on explorations of gender roles and feminism. Her discussion of two Turkish *Driver Nebahat* films (1960 original and a 1970 remake) explores how the character's masculine cross-dressing is social-politically constructed, and reflects the shifting and complex nature of female roles in the 1950s and 1960s. In contrast to the fictional character explored by Ulusoy, Kelly M. O'Donnell examines two young female celebrities, Emma Watson and Miley Cyrus, and their 'practice' of feminism, discussing how their different embodiment of feminism engages with contemporary debates about feminism.

Leaving a Legacy

Concluding the discussion on celebrity and activism are two chapters that focus on celebrities' posthumous images. These celebrities possessed a high celebrity status during their lifetimes. However, since their deaths they have become symbols of activism and philanthropy. Marie Josephine Bennett's chapter discusses how Freddie Mercury, who was reluctant to openly acknowledge his HIV/AIDS status in life, has since become a symbol for HIV/AIDS awareness. Jackie Raphael's chapter explores how Paul Newman's philanthropic activity has created a means for his posthumous image to live on. Both chapters portray the power of a celebrity's brand.

Acknowledgments

The editors wish to thank the Centre for Media and Celebrity Studies (CMCS) and the Centre for Ecological, Social, and Informatics Cognitive Research (ESI.CORE) who sponsored the conference, which inspired this book. They would also like to thank the authors for contributing to the volume and our reviewers – Nathan Farrell, Chuck Carney, Basuli Deb, Josh Nathan, Stephanie Patrick, Andrea Marshall, Nidhi Shrivastava, Kiera Obbard, Rachel Haworth and Andrew Zolides. Thanks also to Professor P David Marshall for providing the Foreword to this volume.

Reference

Rojek, C. (2001). *Celebrity*. London: Reaktion Books Ltd.

PART I:
Approaches to Activism

Offstage humanitarianism: Reality, drama and 'successful misunderstanding'

Carla Rocavert

Abstract: Humanitarianism has become central to celebrity profile management in the 21st century. For actors and artists, balancing 'relatability' with the aspirational features of a life in the spotlight can be greatly assisted by 'offstage' charity work. Itself a kind of media performance that resembles the drama of reality television, philanthropy offers red carpet opportunities and far-reaching media coverage; it can also offset associations with corporate wealth, and even redirect public obsession with a celebrity's private life. While most actor celebrities no doubt believe in their causes, and their advocacy provides much needed exposure, it is worth questioning how their social contributions offstage differ to those onstage. As charity and consumer messages compete for position in the 24-hour news cycle, the interplay between ethics, reality and drama – as it affects audiences' understanding – deserves examination. This chapter uses current research in creativity, reality television and media philosophy to critically discuss issues of media ethics and humanitarianism in the context of contemporary screen stardom in the 21st Century.

Keywords: Reality television, celebrity, charity, drama

Introduction

The current state of celebrity humanitarianism, with all its reported ideological contamination, theatricality, and lack of real effectiveness[1] can be understood as a mode of reality television. From the 'charitainment' (Poniewozik, 2005) of George Clooney and Angelina Jolie's political intervention in warzones, to tax scandals involving churches founded by the Kardashians (Balsamini, Vincent, & Klein, 2016; Cronin, 2014), the spectacle of 'giving' and indeed "the spectatorship of suffering" (Chouliaraki, 2006) continues to play out across numerous media channels around the world. Celebrities from all walks of life are now involved, but for actors and artists specifically, charity engagements are part of what is known as their 'offstage' (Gledhill, 1991, after Dyer, 1986) or publicity work (p. 213). This is the activity in which the performer, instead of bringing characters to life through drama onstage, embodies personas based on the 'real'.

---

[1] See Brockington & Henson, 2014; Chouliaraki, 2006, 2010 & 2011; Dieter & Kumar, 2008; Kapoor, 2012, p. 1; Scott, 2015; Stanford, 2011.

Gledhill (1991) describes the onstage/offstage distinction:

> Stardom proper arises when the offstage or off-screen life of the actor becomes as important as the performed role in the production of a semi-autonomous persona or image…the slippage between the player's performance of a role, and a player's private life suggests an intensification of the process of personalization in which the relation between the emblematic, moral schema of melodrama and social reality is recast. (p. 213)

In charity specifically, the aim is to personalize and emblematize social, political or environmental problems in a way that uses melodrama to convey moral messages. As a number of scholars have already pointed out, this has become problematic because the subjects at issue (the sufferers and the participants) become trivialized, simplified and depicted in ways that promote a misinformed and emotion-laden view of their situation (Dieter & Kumar, 2008; Scott, 2015, p. 450). Furthermore, much like in reality television, a successful misunderstanding takes place. Audiences interpret the construct of giving as real (in other words ethical, altruistic and valuable) without questioning the power structures that underpin the transaction. Behind both reality television and charity is often a corporate advertising project, which in turn, is bolstered and reframed by the 'reality drama' in focus. Not only does the consumerist orientation of activism also reinforce the broader structures and systems that perpetuate inequality (Kapoor, 2012), it can trick the viewer into an inactive, and even "narcissistic disposition" (Chouliaraki, 2010) toward sufferers.

At another end of the entertainment spectrum, artistic drama works toward a different purpose. At its best it can promote the sharing of knowledge, and empower audiences not just to understand, but to empathize. Critically, this does not involve the subplot of selling a product. Rather, actors and creative teams enter the lives of people who are different, with the aim of letting audiences know "what that feels like", as Meryl Streep noted at the 2017 Golden Globe Awards (as cited in Friedman, 2017). Her message contained warnings both about the 'spectacle' of drama for ulterior purposes, and the necessity of mediums such as drama and good journalism to provide audiences with truthful perspectives on the root causes of social problems.

While celebrities do successfully generate exposure[2] (Stanford & Forsyth, 2011) for charities, and their projects are no doubt personally important to them, humanitarianism as a whole is marred by persistent reports of global inequality

---

[2] See especially Leonardo DiCaprio's documentary *Before the Flood*, released in 2016.

and corruption in the 24-hour news cycle. Increasing celebrity activism (Brockington, 2014) has perhaps even coincided with a rise in reports of political and corporate wrongdoing,[3] making it difficult for members of the elite – including celebrities – to escape criticism. Negotiating their own value in an ever-more negative media landscape (Stafford, 2014) it is often stars themselves who become the subject of stories about the mishandling of charity (Birrell, 2012; The Daily Mail, 2010; Baum, 2015; Samuel, 2016), which adds to public confusion and skepticism (Scott, 2015). For the consumer more generally, the lack of access to clear, non-contradictory, non-consumer driven dialogue is indeed resulting in alienation and depoliticization (Kapoor, 2012) in the post-democratic (Crouch, 2004), post-truth (Flood, 2016) era.

Entertainment at large however, is not totally futile. Those that continue their work *onstage* do so with the aim of connecting audiences to humanitarian issues. The effectiveness of such work, where actors meet their "responsibility of the act of empathy" (Streep as cited in Friedman, 2017) and provide a "moral compass" (Belafonte, 2014) should not be overlooked. This chapter discusses humanitarianism both through drama and as drama, seeking to elucidate the distinctions between onstage and offstage humanitarianism in order to redefine activism as a social, rather than an economic, concept. While charitable organizations also serve a role, here the relevant questions pertain to the artists' contribution, and the difference between performances in which reality is understood, and 'productions' where it is manufactured.

The Key Philanthropic Players

Music, sport and film stars have long been engaging in the political sphere. Records show that actors were used as political messengers as far back as in ancient Greece, (Scott, 2015) and it is now with increasing regularity that they appear on behalf of charities (Brockington & Henson, 2014, p. 1). Substantial literature now exists on the major 21st century figures such as Bono, Angelina Jolie and George Clooney. More recently, personalities from other fields such as soccer's Didier Drogba and Mark Zuckerberg (Bentley, Lawton, et al., 2016; Kapoor, 2013; Massing, 2016) have also made headlines. These famous individuals' philanthropic activities – ranging from ambassadorships with the United Nations, to business and government lobbying, to concert shows – have attracted both praise and criticism. As Justin Forsythe, CEO of Save the Children explained to *The Guardian;* "of course celebrity touch isn't everything", but "without the campaigning energies of Bono, Bob Geldof and

---

[3] See Guardian reports on the Panama Papers, 2016, and reports on African trade and poverty (Kar & Spangers, 2014; Sharpless, Jones & Martin, 2014). See also Kapoor (2012, p. 32).

Richard Curtis, for example, I don't believe 46 million more children would be in school today in some of the world's poorest countries" (2011). Even celebrity advocacy critics have recognized the "significant personal time" and "astonishing" press levels achieved for causes (Kapoor, 2012, p. 17; 87).

But with estimated incomes similar or equal to middle and large-size corporations and individual "philanthrocapitalists" (Massing, 2016), celebrities (Brockington & Henson, 2014; Creswell, 2008) – like the charities they represent (Garton, 2016) – remain broadly distrusted by the public. This is no doubt in large part due to scandalous media narratives in mainstream and tabloid news, which in their own way, mirror the melodramatic tropes of reality television. Famous ambassadors tell the public that they are engaged and "putting people first" (Zuckerberg, 2016), but in a different headline may be accused of cheating the system or exploiting their wealth and power. Some of the issues that have plagued more famous givers include: exploitation of orphans by Drogba (Bentley, Lawton, et. al., 2016); Clooney's financial contracts with Nestle (Siegle, 2013); Bono's secret extravagances, tax avoidance (Belfast Telegraph, 2009; Celebs on Yachts, 2015), and wealth management and investment side ventures (Balakrishnan, 2015); major tax benefits for Zuckerberg (Massing, 2016); and indeed the overuse of charity to 'reconstruct' one's image entirely.

Jolie's transformation from Hollywood wild child (Barnes, 2008) to career philanthropist and mother of "transnational" children (Kapoor, 2012, p. 17) is a key example. While her donations have reportedly made a significant difference in various conflict zones (UNHCR, n. d.),[4] evidence of her image "orchestration" (Barnes, 2008) can be seen in: the resemblance her work bears to Audrey Hepburn's role for UNICEF (Chouliaraki, 2010; 2012), endorsement and consumption of luxury products (Cain & Rach, 2016; Lawson 2016), appearances in designer wear at shopping malls with her children (Barsamian, 2016), academic engagements (Ferguson, 2016) and control of paid tabloid stories about her personal life (Barnes, 2008). She is undoubtedly the epitome of transference from onstage to offstage celebrity. Having *become* the humanitarian brand, in more recent press, she continues to dramatize her reality television-like narrative both through histrionic personal episodes, and as transformed humanitarian, mother and rescuer (Associated Press, 2016).

Moreover, charity roles provide insights about the ways public image is now controlled more broadly. Just as philanthropy is useful for corporations wishing to manage their brands and reputations (Massing, 2016), humanitarianism for

---

[4] Angelina Jolie has donated more than $5 million towards the building of schools in locations such as Kenya and Afghanistan (USA for UNHCR, n. d.).

performers provides a means of navigating the balance between 'relatability' and illustriousness, between ordinariness and elitism. As celebrities are also increasingly business minded, both facilitating NGO/corporate partnerships (Brockington & Henson, 2014) and investing in corporations themselves (Nexchange, 2016), charity helps to redirect media attention from the 'wealthy individual' persona. It can also distract audiences from other activities that could be considered sanctimonious. Examples of this include; promoting messages of sustainability and equality whilst travelling by private jet and luxury yacht, deriving incomes from exploitative business models (Mills, 2016),[5] and consuming "sumptuous food and wine" and "spectacular" entertainment at charity balls (Red Ball, 2016) for the ill.

The Co-production of Value between Celebrity, Charity and Consumer

Rose and Woods' research outlines the concept of audience co-production in reality television: "We accept as authentic the fantasy that we co-produce" (Rose & Woods, 2005, p. 295). Following Žižek's analysis of the real (Žižek, 1999, p. 11), they explain how viewers can both trick themselves into believing that media representations of reality are unscripted, and in fact remain aware of the contrived conventions (Rose & Woods, 2005, p. 292). The combination of the spontaneous with the produced provides the viewer with 'drama', grounding the events in reality so as to construct a sense of participation. This highlights what Scott (2015) and Chouliaraki (2006) have described as the "paradox of distance" (Scott, 2015, p, 451) and of "action/inaction" (Chouliaraki, 2006, p. 88). Mediatization enables both proximity and distance, rendering the spectator participant, observer, and also fundamentally, consumer.

It is in this framework that charity can be said to foster successful misunderstanding (Rose & Woods, 2005, p. 292; Žižek, 1999, p. 12 after Lacan). Where reality television audiences willingly buy into what is unreal in order to co-produce an 'authentic' moment (Rose & Woods, 2005, p. 288), audiences of charity donate, or follow celebrity humanitarians, which serves to palliate, rather than address social ills. Not only is the focus more likely to be on the celebrity rather than the issue (Brockington & Henson, 2014, p. 14), but the social, political or environmental *message* becomes part of the broader panorama of reality media and the entertainment industry itself. Ongoing and

---

[5] Beyoncé's sportswear range came under fire in 2016 for exploiting Sri Lankan workers making some of the clothes.

widespread 'participation' is just as (if not far more) likely to be achieved for a naked 'selfie' (Gritt et al., 2016), an *X Factor* episode (Frere-Jones, 2008; Shepherd, 2016), or political sagas echoing through social media bubbles, as seen following the 2016 US election. In each of these highly corporatized entertainments, dialogue about the causes of social ills is subjugated,[6] and sensationalized pseudo-narratives (Boorstin, 1962; Gabler, 1998) around celebrity distance the audience from reality.

When considered as a kind of 'consumerism drama', the action/inaction of mediatized participation in charity is thus ethically problematic on a number of levels. Campaigns such as those fronted by Bono for RED American Express,[7] Gwyneth Paltrow's ambassadorship for donor advised fund *DonorsChoose*[8] and a luxury watch label (Frederique Constant, 2016), and Beyoncé's feminism messages conveyed through deeply personalized, sexualized performances of the self (IVY PARK SS16, 2016), highlight the ambiguity, and even disingenuousness of selling *via* activism. Amid the daily milieu of already unprecedented levels of advertising (Creswell 2008; Johnson, 2014), such hyper-textual entertainments of drama, charity and advertising dilute, rather than raise, critical awareness.

Conclusion

As morality is tied to consumerism, and the dissonance between luxury and poverty, activism and exploitation becomes more opaque, it is easy to forget that many celebrity activists are technically *actors*. While in their second careers they have become business people, political commentators and activists, it remains that 'performance' is what brought them international recognition. The solution to what academics have so far labeled "inauthentic aspirational discourse" (Chouliaraki, 2010) in charity may be found in drawing more attention to the value of the very medium that provided actors a voice in political spheres. Performance has served many other purposes, but one undeniable constant is the successful exposure of the dangers of unfettered power, and the effectiveness of telling the story of the Other. Recent stage and screen works such as Victoria Brittain and Gillian Slovo's *Guantanamo* (2011),

---

[6] A number of scholars have discussed this irony in different ways. See Chouliaraki, 2006, Scott, 2015, p. 251 & p. 452, Kapoor, 2012; Dieter & Kumar, 2008; Richey & Ponte, 2011.

[7] See Richey & Ponte's discussion of the RED American Express card slogan "Has there ever been a better time to shop?" 2011, p. XI.

[8] Cullman & Madoff (2016) explore the under-regulated and unethical rise of donor advised funds in America.

Adam McKay's *The Big Short* (2016), Tom McCarthy's *Spotlight* (2015), Oliver Stone's *Snowden* (2016) and Ken Loach's *I, Daniel Blake* (2016) attest to this. These performances and many others have given audiences meaningful engagement with morality and humanitarianism as a social (Malpas, 2012, p. 7) – rather than an economic – concept. Drama is inherently both dialogical and social.

If it is ultimately the audience that must be empowered to understand their changing world and empathize with sufferers, then it is mediums which counteract the contradictions and ambiguities of mediatized reality that are needed. In their onstage roles, actors are not the privileged individuals who derive wealth from the very structures of inequality and injustice that necessitate humanitarian programs – and thus the proponents of power – but commentators on it. Art, of course, cannot solve the world's problems single-handedly, but as reality entertainment increasingly overshadows the stage that, as Harry Belafonte[9] noted, has long been "the catalyst for social change" (2014), it is with increasing caution that we should view the offstage drama of produced reality, celebrity and charity. Art, on issues of humanity, remains a safer bet than the rest.

Acknowledgments

With sincere thanks to Distinguished Professor Jeff Malpas.

References

Associated Press. (2016, February 17). Angelina Jolie reveals before she adopted Maddox she had no plans for children. *Daily Mail Online.* Retrieved from http://www.dailymail.co.uk/tvshowbiz/article-3451038/AP-Interview-Angelina-Jolie-returns-Cambodia-director.html.

Balakrishnan, A. (2015, September 1). Bono's Facebook stake outearned his music: Report. *CNBC.* Retrieved from http://www.cnbc.com/2015/09/01/bonos-facebook-stake-outearned-his-music-report.html.

Balsamini, D., Vincent, I., & Klein, M. (2016, March 28). Barely any proceeds of Kim Kardashian's eBay auction are actually going to charity. *News.com.au.* Retrieved from http://www.news.com.au/entertainment/celebrity-life/barely-any-proceeds-of-kim-kardashians-ebay-auction-are-actually-going-to-charity/news-story/c272fb5dad70750460aa05cc568204ec.

---

[9] 2014 winner of the Jean Hersholt Humanitarian Award

Barnes, B. (2008, November 21). Angelina Jolie's Carefully Orchestrated Image. *The New York Times*. Retrieved from http://www.nytimes.com/2008/11/21/business/media/21angelina.html?_r=0.

Barsamian, E. (2016, August 16). Angelina Jolie Pitt Wears the Summer Cover-Up to the Mall. *Vogue*. Retrieved from http://www.vogue.com/13466723/angelina-jolie-pitt-saint-laurent-gianvito-rossi-celebrity-mall-style/.

Baum, G. (2015, February 4). Eva Longoria, Two "Philanthropreneurs" and the Dangers of Hollywood Charity: THR Investigates. *The Hollywood Reporter*. Retrieved from http://www.hollywoodreporter.com/features/eva-longoria-two-philanthropreneurs-dangers-769240.

Belafonte, H. (2014, November 9). "Harry Belafonte receives the Jean Hersholt Humanitarian Award at the 2014 Governors Awards." [Youtube]. *2014 Governors Awards*. Retrieved from https://www.youtube.com/watch?v=Yfj6Ja86lCs.

Bentley, P., Lawton, M. & Faulkner, K. (2016, April 14). How football star's luvvie charity exploited orphans: As Drogba faces probe over £1.7million that didn't reach sick Africans, troubling new questions emerge. *Daily Mail Online*. Retrieved from http://www.dailymail.co.uk/news/article-3540739/How-football-star-s-luvvie-charity-exploited-orphans-Drogba-faces-probe-1-7million-didn-t-reach-sick-Africans-troubling-new-questions-emerge.html.

Belfast Telegraph. (2009, February 25). U2 frontman Bono's tax avoidance 'depriving poor'. *Belfast Telegraph*. Retrieved from http://www.belfasttelegraph.co.uk/entertainment/music/news/u2-frontman-bonos-tax-avoidance-depriving-poor-28509721.html.

Birrell, I. (2012, January 27). Haiti and the shaming of the aid zealots: How donated billions have INCREASED poverty and corruption. *The Daily Mail*. Retrieved from http://www.dailymail.co.uk/news/article-2092425/Haiti-earthquake-How-donated-billions-INCREASED-poverty-corruption.html.

Boorstin, D. (1962). *The Image: A Guide to Pseudo-Events in America*. New York, NY: Atheneum.

Brockington, D. (2014). The production and construction of celebrity advocacy in international development. *Third World Quarterly, 35*(1), 88-108. http://dx.doi.org/10.1080/01436597.2014.868987.

Brockington, D. & Henson, S. (2014). Signifying the public: Celebrity advocacy and post-democratic politics. *International Journal of Cultural Studies,18*(4), 1-18.

Cain, D. & Rach, J. (2016, June 1). Inside the majestic Majorcan £2.65million seaside mansion 'bought by Angelina Jolie and Brad Pitt for their extensive property portfolio'. *Daily Mail*. Retrieved from http://www.dailymail.co.uk/tvshowbiz/article-3620729/Jolie-Pitt-s-rumoured-2-65-million-mansion-Hollywood-couple-reportedly-add-majestic-Majorcan-villa-extensive-property-portfolio.html.

Celebs on Yachts staff. (2015). Inside Look: Bono's Secret Yacht is Called Kingdom Come! *Celebs on Yachts.* Retrieved from http://www.celebsonyachts.com/inside-look-bonos-secret-yacht-is-called-kingdom-come/.

Chouliaraki, L. (2006). *The Spectatorship of Suffering.* London, UK: Sage.

Chouliaraki L (2010) Post-humanitarianism: humanitarian communication beyond a politics of pity. *International Journal of Cultural Studies, 13*(2): 107–126.

Chouliaraki, L. (2011). 'Improper distance': towards a critical account of solidarity as irony. *International Journal of Cultural Studies, 14*(4): 363–381.

Chouliaraki L (2012) The theatricality of humanitarianism: a critique of celebrity advocacy. *Communication and Critical/Cultural Studies, 9*(1): 1–21.

Creswell, J. (2008, June 22). Nothing Sells Like Celebrity. *New York Times.* Retrieved from http://www.nytimes.com/2008/06/22/business/media/22celeb.html?_r=0.

Cronin. M. (2014, March 28). Inside Kim Kardashian's Charity Tax Scandal: Tax Documents Reveal How She Funneled Money from EBay Auction to Mom's Church. *Radaronline*. Retrieved from http://radaronline.com/exclusives/2014/03/kim-kardashian-charity-tax-documents-kris-jenner-church/.

Crouch, C. (2004). *Post-Democracy.* Cambridge UK: Polity Press Ltd.

Cullman, L. B., & Madoff, R. (2016, July 14). The Undermining of American Charity. *The New York Review of Books.* Retrieved from http://www.nybooks.com/articles/2016/07/14/the-undermining-of-american-charity/.

Dieter, H. & Kumar, R. (2008). The downside of celebrity diplomacy: The neglected complexity of development. *Global Governance, 14*(3), 259–264.

Dyer, R. (1986). *Heavenly bodies: film stars and society*. New York, NY. St Martin's Press.

Ferguson, K. (2016, May 23). Angelina Jolie appointed as professor at the London School of Economics. *Independent.* Retrieved from http://www.independent.co.uk/news/people/angelina-jolie-appointed-as-professor-at-the-london-school-of-economics-a7043911.html.

Flood, A. (2016, November 15). 'Post-truth' named word of the year by Oxford Dictionaries. *The Guardian.* Retrieved from https://www.theguardian.com/books/2016/nov/15/post-truth-named-word-of-the-year-by-oxford-dictionaries.

Frere-Jones, S. (2008, May 19). Idolatry Everybody's a critic. *The New Yorker.* Retrieved from http://www.newyorker.com/magazine/2008/05/19/idolatry.

Frederique Constant. (2016, May 4). New charity ambassador Gwyneth Paltrow gives her thoughts on the new Delight Automatic in an exclusive interview. *Frederique*

Constant Geneve. Retrieved from https://frederiqueconstant.com/news/new-charity-ambassador-gwyneth-paltrow-gives-her-thoughts-on-the-new-delight-automatic-in-an-exclusive-interview/.

Friedman, M (2017). Here's the full transcript of Meryl Streep's powerful Golden Globes speech. *Harpers Bazaar.* Retrieved from http://www.harpersbazaar.com/culture/film-tv/news/a19828/meryl-street-golden-globes-speech-transcript/.

Gabler, N. (1998). *Life: The Movie: How Entertainment Conquered Reality.* New York, NY: Vintage Books.

Garton, J. (2016). Why has trust in charities been declining? *The Conversation.* Retrieved from http://theconversation.com/why-has-trust-in-charities-been-declining-49825.

Gledhill, C. (1991). Signs of Melodrama. In C. Gledhill (Ed.), *Stardom: Industry of Desire.* New York: Routledge.

Gritt, E. & staff writers. (2016, March 8). Kim Kardashian shares nude selfie in 'desperate attempt to stay relevant'. *News.com.au.* Retrieved from http://www.news.com.au/entertainment/celebrity-life/kim-kardashian-shares-nude-selfie-in-desperate-attempt-to-stay-relevant/news-story/d671a95cec1f9aa3b56d1d25438bd974.

Holmes, S. (2005). "Off guard, Unkempt, Unready?": Deconstructing Contemporary Celebrity in heat Magazine, *Continuum: Journal of Media and Cultural Studies, 19*(1), 21-38.

IVY PARK SS16. (2016). Beyoncé 'Where is your park'. *YouTube.* Retrieved from https://www.youtube.com/watch?v=mA1Wp1kfDfE.

Johnson, S. (2014). New Research Sheds Light on Daily Ad Exposures. *SJ Insights.* Retrieved from https://sjinsights.net/2014/09/29/new-research-sheds-light-on-daily-ad-exposures/.

Kapoor, I. (2012). *Celebrity Humanitarianism: The Ideology of Global Charity.* New York, NY: Routledge.

Global Financial Integrity. (2014). *Illicit Financial Flows from Developing Countries: 2003-2012.* Washington, DC: Kar, D. & Spangers, J. Retrieved from http://www.gfintegrity.org/wp-content/uploads/2014/12/Illicit-Financial-Flows-from-Developing-Countries-2003-2012.pdf.

Lawson, R. (2016, April 22). Brad Pitt and Angelina Jolie's $21,000/Month London Mansion Is an Inspiration to All Business Travelers. *Vanity Fair.* Retrieved from http://www.vanityfair.com/hollywood/2016/04/brad-pitt-and-angelina-jolie-london-mansion.

Malpas, J. (2012). The Demise of Ethics. In M. Schwartz & H. Harris (Eds.), *Applied Ethics: Remembering Patrick Primeaux (Research in Ethical Issues in*

Organizations, Volume 8) (pp. 29-45). Bingly, UK: Emerald Group Publishing Limited.

Massing, M. (2016, January 14). How to Cover the One Percent. *New York Review of Books*. Retrieved from http://www.nybooks.com/articles/2016/01/14/how-to-cover-the-one-percent/.

Mills, J. (2016, May 7). Exposed: Sweatshop 'slaves' earning just 44p an hour making 'empowering' Beyonce clobber. *The Sun* https://www.thesun.co.uk/archives/news/1176905/exposed-sweatshop-slaves-earning-just-44p-an-hour-making-empowering-beyonce-clobber/.

Nexchange. (2016). 6 celebrities who are also prolific venture capital investors. *Nexchange*. Retrieved from https://nexchange.com/article/8520.

Poniewozik, J. (2005, December 19). The Year of Charitainment. *TIME*. Retrieved from http://content.time.com/time/magazine/article/0,9171,1142281,00.html.

Red Ball. (2016). Retrieved from https://www.redball.com.au.

Richey, L. A., & Ponte S. (2011). *Brand Aid: Shopping Well to Save the World*. Minneapolis, USA: University of Minnesota Press.

Rose, R. L., & Wood, S. L. (2005). Paradox and the consumption of authenticity through reality television. *Journal of Consumer Research*, *32*(2), 284–296. doi:10.1086/432238.

Samuel, H. (2016, September 1). Leonardo DiCaprio urged to repay donations tied to massive Malaysian 'embezzlement scheme'. *The Telegraph*. Retrieved from http://www.telegraph.co.uk/news/2016/08/31/leonardo-dicaprio-urged-to-repay-donations-tied-to-massive-malay/.

Scott, M. (2015). The role of celebrities in mediating distant suffering. *International Journal of Cultural Studies, 18*(4), 449–466.

Scott, M. (2015). Ancient Greece: The Greatest Show on Earth (1of3): Democrats (with Michael Scott). *BBC*. Retrieved from https://www.youtube.com/watch?v=FqnBBjC_8no.

Sharpless, N., Jones, T. & Martin, C. (2014). Honest Accounts? The true story of Africa's billion dollar losses. *Health Poverty Action*. Retrieved from https://www.healthpovertyaction.org/speaking-out/honest-accounts/.

Shepherd, J. (2016, August 28). The X Factor 2016 ratings hit a 10-year low as 6.8m viewers tune in for first episode. *The Independent*. Retrieved from http://www.independent.co.uk/arts-entertainment/tv/news/the-x-factor-2016-ratings-hit-ten-year-low-as-68-million-viewers-tune-in-for-first-episode-a7213796.html.

Siegle, L. (2013, July 17). George Clooney tastes sustainability in Nespresso coffee. *The Guardian*. Retrieved from http://www.theguardian.com/environment/blog/2013/jul/17/george-clooney-nespresso-coffee-ad.

Stafford, T. (2014, July 28). Psychology: why bad news dominates the headlines. *BBC*. Retrieved from http://www.bbc.com/future/story/20140728-why-is-all-the-news-bad.

Stanford, P. & Forsythe, J. (2011, June 26). Are celebrities a help or hindrance to charities? *The Guardian*. Retrieved from http://www.theguardian.com/commentisfree/2011/jun/26/celebrity-ambassadors-charities-debate.

The Daily Mail staff (2010). Bono's ONE foundation under fire for giving little over 1% of funds to charity. *The Daily Mail*. Retrieved from http://www.dailymail.co.uk/news/article-1314543/Bonos-ONE-foundation-giving-tiny-percentage-funds-charity.html.

The Guardian (2016). *Panama Papers*. Retrieved from https://www.theguardian.com/news/series/panama-papers.

USA for UNHCR (n. d.). Angelina Jolie Pitt – UNHCR Special Envoy. Retrieved from http://www.unrefugees.org/angelina-jolie-unhcr-special-envoy/.

Žižek, S. (1999). The undergrowth of enjoyment: how popular culture can serve as an introduction to Lacan. In E. & E. Wright (Eds.), *The Žižek Reader* (pp. 11-36). Oxford: Blackwell.

Zuckerberg, M. (April 30, 2016) Facebook's Zuckerberg: We Must Put People First. *FacebookF8 Developer's Conference San Francisco*. Retrieved from http://www.bloomberg.com/news/videos/b/3a0951f8-8109-459f-8ffc-0025bb85334e.

The Emergence of the 'Super-Celebrity Activist': George Clooney and Angelina Jolie

Sally Totman

Abstract: Given the number of social and political issues prevalent in the world it is surprising how few A-list Hollywood actors involve themselves with these issues. Two celebrities stand out from the crowd in this arena: George Clooney and Angelina Jolie. As members of the prestigious Council on Foreign Relations (CFR), which is the most influential foreign policy think tank in the United States (Lobe, 2005), Clooney and Jolie have used their celebrity status to highlight issues in the Sudan, and refugees, respectively. This paper explores the history and activism of these two celebrities and how through utilizing their celebrity, political connections, and even business partnerships, these celebrities have effected real change for thousands of people and in the process have themselves transformed into 'super-celebrity activists'.

Keywords: Celebrity, Angelina Jolie, George Clooney, Celebrity-Political Magnification.

On May 16, 2016 Angelina Jolie joined notables such as former British secret intelligence chief Sir Richard Dearlove and the United Nations High Commissioner for Refugees, Filippo Grandi, to highlight the global migration and refugee crisis (BBC, 2016). This was the latest in a series of speeches by Jolie in her role as the Special Envoy for the UNHCR to draw international attention to the plight of refugees across the globe. Her first major speech in this new role was in April 2015 to the United Nations Security Council (UNSC) on the Syrian Refugee Crisis (UNHCR, 2015).

Jolie has long been involved with refugee advocacy and was a UNHCR Goodwill Ambassador from 2001-2012. During this period she performed over 50 field missions and cemented her role as an influential advocate on refugee and displacement matters (UNHCR, 2016). In April 2012, Jolie was appointed to the UNHCR Special Envoy role. In this portfolio she focuses on major crises that result in mass population displacements, undertaking advocacy and representing UNHCR and the High Commissioner at the diplomatic level. She also engages with decision-makers on global displacement issues. Through this work, she has helped contribute to the vital process of finding solutions for people forced to flee their homes (UNHCR, 2016).

Jolie's activism originated in 2001 when she was exposed to the plight of refugees while filming in Cambodia. She followed this awakening with a series of visits to refugee camps in Sierra Leone, Tanzania, Pakistan and several other war-torn countries. These visits were recounted in her book *Notes from My*

Travels (Jolie, 2003) and was released to coincide with her film *Beyond Borders* (Campbell, 2003), which was a dramatic and romance-inspired film drawing attention to humanitarian concerns in Africa.

Whilst there is a tradition of celebrities using their status to draw attention to specific causes (Wilson, 2014), what differentiates Jolie from other celebrities who are UN Goodwill Ambassadors or donate money and time to causes is that she has closely aligned her work and her activism. This has occurred through writing, directing, producing and acting in films that draw attention to humanitarian issues. For example in 2011, Jolie's directorial feature debut *In the Land of Blood and Honey* (Jolie, 2011) depicted a love story between a Serb soldier and a Bosnian prisoner of war during the 1992 conflict. In an interview about the film Jolie was asked whether famous people have a responsibility to draw attention to a cause or social issue and she replied:

> I tend to not think about it as a celebrity thing, but as a human thing. Celebrities just have a louder voice... I have been fortunate enough to have success, be able to shine a light into the camera a little more, financially build something, support people or programs. (Lee, 2012)

Jolie's work in this arena is a prime example of Celebrity-Political Magnification (Totman & Marshall, 2015) whereby celebrities use their prominence to magnify specific issues, which in turn increases their own celebrity status. Jolie has regularly been named Hollywood's highest-paid actress by Forbes (2016) and she has made her economic success qualitatively distinctive by spending, quite openly and visibly, much of her own money on various humanitarian projects. Many of Jolie's projects are quite ambitious in scope including such ventures as building schools and centers to treat children suffering with HIV, in countries including Afghanistan, Cambodia, Ethiopia, and Kenya. Jolie's humanitarian work has been recognized by the film industry, as the recipient of the 2013 Jean Hersholt Humanitarian Award from the Academy of Motion Pictures Arts and Sciences. Her activism has even been legitimized beyond her home country. In 2014 she became the first American woman to be appointed an Honorary Dame Commander of the Order of St Michael and St George (DCMG) by Queen Elizabeth II; an award in recognition of her services to the United Kingdom's foreign policy and campaigning to end sexual violence in war zones.

Like Angelina Jolie, George Clooney has made and starred in a host of films with political messages such as *Three Kings* (Russell, 1999), *Syriana* (Gaghan, 2005), *Good Night, and Good Luck* (Clooney, 2005), and *The Ides of March* (Clooney, 2011) with the last two films also directed by him. In addition, Clooney has produced other political films such as *Argo* (Affleck, 2012). Like Jolie, Clooney has shifted from actor to director, producer and screenwriter of films that have real political messages. Clooney's role in making politically-inspired films has consolidated his persona as a politically aware and involved individual, and has also made Clooney one of the most successful players in the film industry. He is the only person ever to be nominated for Academy Awards in six categories with most of these coming from his politically-inspired work (Hammond, 2013).

Similar to Jolie, Clooney has augmented his film work with official international humanitarian roles. Clooney has been one of the United Nations' Messenger of Peace and focused most of his advocacy on the Darfur conflict in Sudan. Throughout the last decade Clooney has worked to raise public and international awareness about the humanitarian crisis in Darfur. He first drew attention to the issue when he spoke at the 'Save Darfur' rally in Washington DC in 2006 and subsequently made a TV documentary with his father *A Journey to Darfur* (Herskowitz, 2006). He narrated and produced the documentary *Sand and Sorrow* (Freedman, 2007) and appeared in the documentary film *Darfur Now* (Braun, 2007). In 2012 Clooney and his father were arrested for civil disobedience outside the Sudanese Embassy in Washington. Clooney stated that he intended to be arrested when he planned the protest to draw attention to the atrocities taking place in Sudan (Devereaux, 2012). Certainly Clooney's 2014 marriage to renowned human rights lawyer Amal Alamuddin adds further weight to his interest and commitment to human rights. This is another example of the Celebrity-Political Magnification loop whereby choices in his personal life add weight and credibility to his public works.

Of course, there has been significant criticism of Clooney's efforts in effecting real change in Sudan (Shearlaw, 2014). Nevertheless, Clooney describes his work and visits to Sudan as the only thing he can to help the situation, by using his celebrity to highlight the problems there:

> The reason I come is not because I'm a policy guy and not because I'm a soldier and not because I can do anything except get this on TV and in the newspapers…The thing that's frustrating and disappointing – and you in the news organizations know this better than anybody – is that the assumption is always: 'Well, if we know, then we do something about it.' And that just isn't true. I mean we knew about Rwanda. We knew about Bosnia. We knew. But there was plausible deniability. So we're going to try and keep it loud enough that at least they can't say they didn't know. (Perry, 2014)

To this end Clooney has written opinion editorials on Sudan for the New York Times (Clooney, Prendergast, & Kumar, 2015) and CNN (Clooney, Kumar, & Prendergast, 2015) and founded the Satellite Sentinel Project (SSP) in 2010, which claims to be "the first sustained public effort to systematically monitor and report on potential hotspots and threats to human security in near real-time. SSP synthesizes evidence from satellite imagery, data pattern analysis, and ground sourcing to produce reports" (Satellite Sentinel Project, 2016).

Clooney has also used his celebrity endorsement of Nespresso to publicize the crisis in South Sudan. The project has been described as being at the "nexus of celebrity, cause and commerce" (Baker, 2015) with Nespresso investing via Non-Governmental Organizations (NGOs) in coffee farms in the emerging state and resulting in the country's first ever non-oil export to Europe (Baker, 2015).

Clooney and Jolie's humanitarian work came together in 2007 when Jolie visited refugees from Darfur in a UNHCR Camp in Chad and donated, through her charity The Jolie-Pitt Foundation, US$1 million (UNHCR, 2007). This linkage of causes is not surprising given both Jolie and Clooney are members of the prestigious and influential Council on Foreign Relations (CFR), which according to its website is "an independent, nonpartisan membership organization, think tank, and publisher" (Council on Foreign Relations, 2016). To be eligible to join this elite organization, candidates must be nominated in writing by a current CFR member and seconded by a minimum of three other individuals. Membership is restricted to US citizens (and permanent residents who have applied to become citizens) and members are required to pay annual dues of hundreds of dollars. The membership roster (2014) reads as a Who's Who of the United States' most rich and powerful including academics, high-profile lawyers, leading bankers, prominent media notables, senior politicians and more than a dozen former Secretaries of State, former CIA Directors and senior members of the intelligence community; and a very select few of Hollywood's elite including Jolie and Clooney. Through the CFR Jolie and Clooney are able to influence US Foreign Policy through the David Rockefeller Studies Program (2016), which is the CFR's 'think tank' and makes recommendations to the presidential administration and diplomatic community, testifies before Congress, provides media briefings, and publishes on foreign policy issues.

It is important to highlight what an elite and powerful foreign policy organization the CFR is in terms of shaping US foreign policy. It is not an organization that seeks publicity or needs celebrity endorsements. In fact, the inclusion of celebrities is something the CFR avoids (hence the prohibitive membership admission hurdles) but 'serious celebrities' like Clooney and Jolie are included as a result of their earnest commitment to their respective humanitarian causes.

Both Clooney and Jolie are easy to critique when they move into these clearly political realms. Their public identities are always a mix of meanings. Clooney for instance is known widely as a practical joker, which is often discussed in interviews and the media (Smith, 2016). Clooney has been twice proclaimed (in 1997 and 2006) as the "sexiest man alive" by People magazine (Kirby, 2014) and at least for much of his adult life, he was a visible womanizer. These kinds of extensions outside of his work as an actor and director point to a superficiality that can jar with such an individual dealing with serious and important issues. Likewise, Jolie's beauty has been calibrated as the "sexiest" on the planet in 2007 by Esquire (Sager, 2013) among other rankings. Her relationship with Brad Pitt and her previous relationships have presented interesting and sometimes soap-operatic messages to an international public that are quite different from her political and humanitarian work (The Judiciary Report, 2010).

What one has to realize in observing these international stars' political and humanitarian work is that their star personas are a complex mix of private and public meanings. Presenting oneself for the camera in fictional roles by the very nature of our entertainment cultures is often revealing something private and intimate. Likewise, the interviews and promotions that surround these films and productions are equally designed to reveal the personal. But, at least for individuals like Jolie and Clooney these are incomplete identities. They are bridging the gaps in their own identities by this work: they have other concerns and other personal dimensions that they are expressing. These more political forays are well-thought through and identify strategic forms of public identity.

Jolie and Clooney set themselves apart from the typical celebrity because of the breadth, scope and longevity of their political involvement. Even other notable celebrity activists such as Madonna or Kanye West who have also participated in 'activist work' around refugees and Africa are not operating on the same level. It is not just the photo opportunity visits to Sudan and refugee camps or the use of their celebrity status to bring a spotlight to humanitarian issues that is important. Rather, it is the combination of this work plus their professional endeavors in politically charged films, and their involvement at the highest level of foreign policy shaping that sets them apart from other celebrities with more tokenistic activist inclinations. Moreover, this comprehensive suite of involvement becomes a positive feedback loop that reinforces the commitment Jolie and Clooney are seen to have as humanitarian champions. At this point it becomes logical rather than sensational to have them providing briefings to the United Nations and the CFR on their areas of humanitarian expertise.

As a result, Jolie and Clooney are now more than celebrities and more than high-profile celebrity activists. They are considered serious players by the political establishment and experts in their humanitarian fields. This in turn reinforces their credentials as celebrities who care and who understand how to use their celebrity power to shine light on otherwise forgotten issues. Certainly their involvement with the CFR elevates them to a higher plane of celebrity activism. It is important to note the CFR normally shies away from celebrities and the exceptions made for Jolie and Clooney demonstrate they are considered distinctive enough to be included in the membership roster.

It is not just on the ground in the Middle East or in high-level government think-tanks where Jolie and Clooney are effecting change. In August 2016, the highly prestigious Georgetown University named Jolie as a visiting professor lecturing on women, peace and security (Dostis, 2016) following her visiting professorship at the London School of Economics in the United Kingdom (Dostis, 2016). Clooney has had formal discussions with Germany's Chancellor Angela Merkel and US President Barack Obama discussing the humanitarian crisis in the Middle East, brainstorming potential solutions (Child, 2016). This high-level endorsement of their work by the United Nations, CFR and other prestigious institutions and parties is enough to recognize that their humanitarian work deserves more respect and less cynicism than is often leveled against them in tabloids and the popular press.

Clooney and Jolie are providing vital information and knowledge bridges that have had tangible and real effects on aspects of our contemporary world that are particularly challenging. As they express it, their identities draw attention. However, they are not content to just use their celebrity status to draw attention. Through their multi-faceted approaches, they are achieving real and meaningful change for thousands of people in the world.

What this chapter highlights is the difference between a 'standard celebrity activist' who uses their fame to draw attention to a cause, or causes, and a 'super-celebrity activist' who not only uses their celebrity to draw attention to a cause but, becomes a recognized expert in the area of their cause and a leading authority in the area. Moreover, these 'super-celebrities' have features that enhance and magnify their expertise and credibility as outlined in the examination of the work of Clooney and Jolie. Figures 1 and 2 exemplify this distinction.

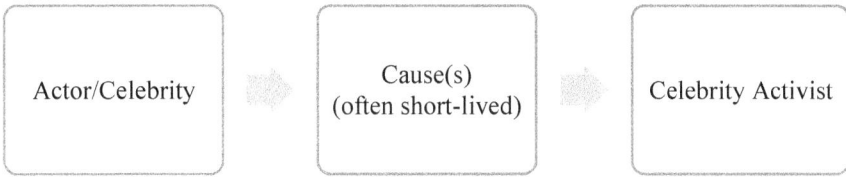

Fig. 1. The standard Celebrity Activist

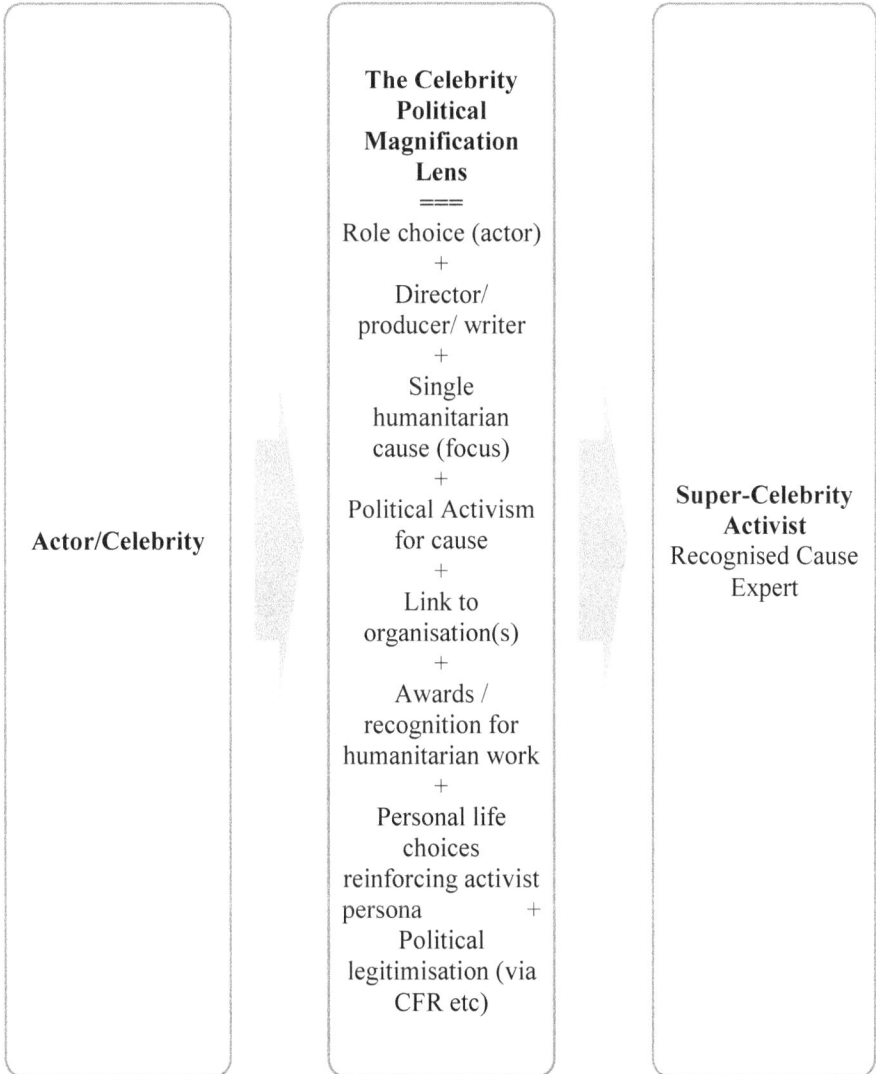

Fig. 2. The Super-Celebrity Activist

What distinguishes the 'super-celebrity' is the additional layers of interrelated activity and commitment. It is not just being an actor with a cause but, being an actor with a cause that influences their acting role choices, which also expands into directing, producing, and writing films related to this activism. Additionally, associations with legitimate organizations like the UNHCR or the Council of Foreign Relations, and making life choices that are consistent with these activities – such as adopting refugee children or marrying a human rights' lawyer – cements their position. Moreover, the process of Celebrity-Political Magnification leads to the celebrity becoming a legitimate spokesperson and authority in their chosen cause and being asked to brief other experts.

The super-celebrity, such as Clooney or Jolie, is a rare entity but in a time where 'fame' and 'celebrity' and 'star' are terms that are often over-used it is important to differentiate the level of Celebrity-Political Magnification that Clooney and Jolie have undergone and to recognize that their commitment and high-level work in their fields outside of Hollywood are in a category all of their own. It is important to highlight that their work is not just about increasing their celebrity status, but their efforts have had a positive impact across the globe for many thousands of disadvantaged people and will no doubt continue to do so.

References

Affleck, B. (Director). (2012). *Argo* [Motion Picture].

Baker, A. (2015, June 12). Why George Clooney is Supporting Coffee Farming in South Sudan. *Time*. Retrieved from http://time.com/3918857/george-clooney-south-sudan/.

BBC. (2016, May 16). Angelina Jolie Pitt: Refugee system breaking down. Retrieved from BBC: http://www.bbc.com/news/world-europe-36303688.

Braun, T. (Director). (2007). *Darfur Now* [Motion Picture].

Campbell, M. (Director). (2003). *Beyond Borders* [Motion Picture].

Child, B. (2016, February 13). George Clooney meets Angela Merkel and backs Germany's support for refugees. *The Guardian*. Retrieved from https://www.theguardian.com/film/2016/feb/12/george-clooney-meets-angela-merkel-germany-support-refugees.

Clooney, G. (Director). (2005). *Good Night, and Good Luck* [Motion Picture].

Clooney, G. (Director). (2011). *The Ides of March* [Motion Picture].

Clooney, G., Kumar, A., & Prendergast, J. (2015, June 25). George Clooney: Sanctions threats not enough in South Sudan. *CNN.* Retrieved from http://edition.cnn.com/2015/06/24/opinions/clooney-kumar-sudan-action/.

Clooney, G., Prendergast, J., & Kumar, A. (2015, February 25). George Clooney on Sudan's Rape of Darfur. *The New York Times.* Retrieved from http://www.nytimes.com/2015/02/26/opinion/george-clooney-on-sudans-rape-of-darfur.html?_r=0.

Council on Foreign Relations. (2014). Membership Roster. *Council of Foreign Relations.* Retrieved from http://i.cfr.org/content/about/annual_report/ar_2014/Sectional_PDFs/Membership_Roster2014.pdf.

Council on Foreign Relations. (2016). About. *Council on Foreign Relations.* Retrieved from http://www.cfr.org/about/.

Council on Foreign Relations. (2016). Think Tank. *Council on Foreign Relations.* Retrieved from http://www.cfr.org/thinktank/.

Devereaux, R. (2012, March 17). George Clooney arrested in planned protest at Sudanese embassy. *The Guardian.* Retrieved from https://www.theguardian.com/world/2012/mar/16/george-clooney-arrested-sudanese-embassy.

Dostis, M. (2016, August 5). Angelina Jolie to teach peace studies at Georgetown University. *New York Daily News.* Retrieved from http://www.nydailynews.com/entertainment/gossip/angelina-jolie-teach-georgetown-university-article-1.2740326?cid=bitly.

Forbes. (2016). Lists. Retrieved from Forbes: http://www.forbes.com/lists/.

Freedman, P. (Director). (2007). *Sand and Sorrow* [Motion Picture].

Gaghan, S. (Director). (2005). *Syriana* [Motion Picture].

Hammond, P. (2013). OSCARS: Is George Clooney Now King Of The Academy Awards? *Deadline.* Retrieved from http://deadline.com/2013/02/oscars-george-clooney-king-academy-awards-436446/.

Herskowitz, L. (Director). (2006). *A Journey to Darfur* [Motion Picture].

Jolie, A. (2003). *Notes from My Travels: Visits with Refugees in Africa, Cambodia, Pakistan and Ecuador*. New York: Pocket Books.

Jolie, A. (Director). (2011). *In the Land of Blood and Honey* [Motion Picture].

Kirby, I. (2014, November 19). The good, the bad and the ugly! A look back at People's Sexiest Man Alive winners over the years... as 28th recipient is announced. *Daily Mail Austraila*. Retrieved from http://www.dailymail.co.uk/tvshowbiz/article-2840313/A-look-People-s-Sexiest-Man-Alive-winners-years-28th-recipient-announced.html.

Lee, Y. (2012). Angelina Jolie: 'In The Land Of Blood And Honey' Inspired Great Fear, Great Emotion. *Huffington Post*. Retrieved from http://www.huffingtonpost.com/2012/03/27/angelina-jolie-in-the-land-of-blood-and-honey_n_1380144.html.

Lobe, J. (2005). Realist's Rule? *Inter Press Service*. Retrieved from http://www.ipsnews.net/2005/08/politics-us-realists-rule/.

Perry, A. (2014, October). George Clooney, South Sudan and How the World's Newest Nation Imploded. *Newsweek*. Retrieved from http://www.newsweek.com/2014/10/10/george-clooney-south-sudan-how-worlds-newest-nation-imploded-274547.html.

Russell, D. O. (Director). (1999). *Three Kings* [Motion Picture].

Sager, M. (2013, October 7). Angelina Jolie: The Sexiest Woman Alive 2004. *Esquire*. Retrieved from http://www.esquire.com/entertainment/g1603/angelina-jolie-photos-1104/.

Satellite Sentinel Project. (2016). Our Story. Retrieved from Satellite Sentinel Project: http://www.satsentinel.org/our-story.

Shearlaw, M. (2014, December 11). What happened to Darfur after George Clooney came to town? *The Guardian*. Retrieved from http://www.theguardian.com/world/2014/dec/11/-sp-george-cloony-darfur-what-next.

Smith, P. (2016, March 4). Watch out, Clooney's about! George's 10 most annoying pranks. *The Telegraph*. Retrieved from http://www.telegraph.co.uk/film/hail-caesar/george-clooney-best-pranks-jokes/.

The Judiciary Report. (2010, August 3). Angelina Jolie's Obsession With Blood. *THe Judiciary Report*. Retrieved from http://www.judiciaryreport.com/angelina_jolie_obsession_with_blood.htm.

Totman, S., & Marshall, P. D. (2015). Real/reel politics and popular culture. *Celebrity Studies*, 6(4), 603-606. doi: 10.1080/19392397.2015.1092214.

UNHCR. (2007, May 10). Jolie-Pitt Foundation donates US$1 million to groups working in Darfur. Retrieved from UNHCR: http://www.unhcr.org/news/latest/2007/5/464348172/jolie-pitt-foundation-donates-us1-million-groups-working-darfur.html.

UNHCR. (2015, April 24). United Nations Security Council (7433rd Meeting), Open Briefing on the Humanitarian Situation in Syria, Remarks by Angelina Jolie Pitt, UNHCR Special Envoy for Refugee Issues. New York, 24 April 2015. Remarks at the UN Security Council. Retrieved from UNHCR: http://www.unhcr.org/553a459d6.html.

UNHCR. (2016). Special Envoy Angelina Jolie Pitt. Retrieved from UNHCR: http://www.unhcr.org/special-envoy-angelina-jolie-pitt.html.

Wilson, J. (2014). Stardom, Sentimental Education and the Shaping of Global Citizens. Cinema Journal, 53(2), 27-49.

The Silent DisCo: Celebrity, Disability and 'Rights Not Charity'

Ellen Finlay and Louise St Guillaume

Abstract. Through structured interaction with fans, commonly referred to as 'meet and greets', musician Taylor Swift fosters the identity of a celebrity who has a sincere interest in the lives and livelihoods of her fans. Coverage of selected fans, particularly those focusing on fans with disability, generate publicity for Swift and allow the fans to be a part of defining Swift's identity as a 'good', accessible and charitable celebrity. Such 'good' work by Swift is undermined however, by her perpetuation of individualist models of disability. Individualist models reduce the relational nature of disability to biologically determined impairment and reproduce charitable narratives of disability; these views however, are criticized by disability advocates and scholars. This is because individualist and charity models are problematic for pursuing structural change and realizing human rights consistent with the United Nations' Disability Convention (DisCO). The DisCo is underpinned by a socially constructed understanding of disability and representation. In this regard, social barriers and individual remedies are not means of redress, instead individualist notions further compound the subordination of 'disability' to ableist hegemony. In the context of disability advocacy; better realizing human rights and dignity ought to be at the center of 'good' celebrity-fan interaction. For as outlined in the DisCo mainstreaming the human rights of people with disability as equal members of human society is imperative to a more just society. What remains to be seen is whether the elevated status of the celebrity is commensurable with an equal rights based approach to fan engagement.

Keywords: Celebrity, disability, human rights

Introduction

Taylor Swift is represented in the media as philanthropic and charitable and has received various accolades on this basis. For example, in 2012 Swift received Nickelodeon's Big Help Award "in recognition of her extensive philanthropic endeavors" (Swift, 2012). For four consecutive years Swift has also topped the Dosomething.org's 'Celebs Gone Good' list (Davis, 2013) and extensively donates to charities (Look to the Stars, 2016). This representation of Taylor Swift as 'generous', 'charitable', 'inspiring' and 'good' is a sentiment echoed by Swift's celebrity friends (Weatherby, 2016) and many fans who feel 'close' to Swift through her acts of support and generosity. One of the ways in which Swift engages with her fans, particularly fans with disability, is through orchestrated fan meet and greets. These meetings however, can perpetuate the individual model of disability because the meeting is often catalyzed through a foregrounding of impairment. These meetings also raise questions about the capacity to generate social or structural change for people with disability. Because of the focus on the individual, broader systemic or systematic reform is not generated.

Challenging structural barriers is important for consistency with the social model of disability, which was developed by the disability movement and disability studies scholars. The social model seeks to change society in order to accommodate people living with impairment; it does not seek to change persons with impairment to accommodate society. It supports the view that people with disability have a right to be fully participating citizens on an equal basis with others (People with Disability Australia (PWDA), 2010-2016).

While the individual fan with disability experiences 'joy' at having met Swift, it is inconsistent with the social model because the interaction does not translate into broader structural change that is required to contribute to advocating for people with disability. Advocacy is important because it is about "acting, speaking or writing to promote, protect and defend the human rights of people with disability" (Disability Advocacy Resource Unit (DARU), 2016). However, questions are raised through the meet and greet about whether advocacy and structural change can be achieved. This is because though the celebrity may recognize equality and human rights, in a context of problematic media representations of people with disability and the elevated position from which the celebrity approaches the meet and greet, the perpetuation of problematic representations of people with disability and the promotion of the celebrity on the basis of such 'generosity' is possible. As such, this chapter explores the capacity for structural change to occur through fan meet and greets for people with disability and questions whether the hierarchies operating between ability and disability, and celebrity and fan, reproduce dynamics which perpetuate the oppression of people with disability in these interactions. Given that part of van Krieken's definition of celebrity relates "celebrity … [to] a quality or status characterized by a capacity to attract attention" (2012, p. 10), it appears unlikely that the wider dynamics of celebrity would subvert the actions of the celebrity to privilege broader social change.

Through exploring the image of Taylor Swift as a 'generous' celebrity, Swift becomes a vehicle for analyzing how celebrity interactions with fans are represented in the media, particularly fan meet and greets. This chapter will argue that this interaction between fan and celebrity cannot bring about structural reform as it operates within dual power hierarchies. This means that advocacy cannot be achieved through individual acts of celebrity-fan charity. This is because these interactions operate within the "self-producing 'perpetual motion' character of attention capital" meaning that "the established celebrity gains even more attention" and the fan, though "bask[ing] in the glow of the celebrity" (van Krieken, 2012, p. 61), does not experience change as consistent with the social model and human rights. This chapter will begin by briefly explaining the core models central to disability scholarship. It will then examine key existing literature about representations of disability, music and charity. Finally, it will apply these models to fan meet and greets between Taylor Swift and fans with disability.

The Individual Model and the Social Model

Key models important to understanding the operationalization of 'disability' in this chapter are the individual model and the social model of disability. The individual model includes the personal tragedy theory of disability and the medical model of disability (Oliver, 1996). The medical model understands disability as a 'problem' to be fixed within the individual. The medical profession in this model assumes a position of power and are seen as 'experts' on disability, assessing, diagnosing, managing, controlling, treating and curing disabled bodies (Humpage, 2007). The medical model is not consistent with recognizing the equal worth of people with disability since it positions them as incomplete or inferior in comparison with the able-bodied and this provides the basis for ableist hegemony. Furthermore, part of what Oliver (1996) has termed the 'individual model' also contains the personal tragedy theory of disability, which is relevant to this chapter and celebrity-fan interaction. The personal tragedy theory invokes discourses of pity, sympathy and the need for able-bodied charity, simultaneously silencing the voices of people with disability and stigmatizing 'disabled bodies'.

These individualist understandings of disability place disabled bodies into a power relationship that objectifies disabled bodies, subsumes the expertise and agency of people with disability, whilst concomitantly constructing people with disability as subhuman. The social model of disability, which developed in response to the medical model alternatively makes a distinction between impairment as the bodily dimension and disability as a "socially generated system of discrimination" (Meekosha & Shuttleworth, 2009, p. 50) that a person with impairment operates within. That is, disability is not a biological fact but is a socially constructed phenomenon resulting in the privileging of the 'able' body to the exclusion or marginalization of non-normative bodies. In this regard the social model has been described as empowering for people with impairments because it shifts disability away from an individualized, personal problem instead locating disability as a problem with the society's attitudes and social environments.

The social model however, has been criticized for failing to reflect the everyday experience of people with disability, which includes the lived experience of impairment (Shakespeare, 2006). In particular, by focusing on disability instead of impairment, the social model falls short of examining the role of impairment, such as chronic pain, in restricting the participation of people with disability in daily life, as well as the conceptual difficulty in maintaining the independence of 'disability' from 'impairment' (2006). In addition, it is contested whether the social model can encapsulate the varied experiences of persons with disability in a comprehensive manner. However, Oliver, who coined the term 'social model', has defended the social model from such claims (see Oliver, 2013). He frames the social model as a useful "tool to improve peoples' lives" (p. 1025). Additionally, he argues the social model acts as a means for maintaining the unity of a collective political identity for people with disability despite a range of life experiences and lived conditions. The effectiveness of such a political move was seen at the level of the international community when the United Nations (UN) adopted the social model to inform the Convention on the Rights of Persons with Disabilities (CRPD) in 2006. The UNCRPD was the result of lengthy negotiations not only between states, but also people with disability and representative organizations. Kayess and French (2008) suggest that the implementation of the Disability Convention (the 'DisCo') has been framed by both government and non-government organizations, as a partnership between the UN and people with disability globally through the lens of 'nothing about us, without us'. The UNCRPD "seeks to redress the physical and social barriers…confronting people with disability…" instead promoting "their full participation and recognition in civil, political, economic, social, and cultural life" (Kayess & Forgarty, 2007, p. 22).[1] Thus, its adoption as a tool informing the 'DisCo', a mechanism for the human rights of people with disability, is why the model is employed in this chapter.

Celebrity, Music, Charity and Disability

Despite such international developments aiming to reframe disability, drawing on disability scholarship, Richardson (2012) highlights the continuing centrality of the medical model in popular culture. Richardson (2012) identifies three stereotypical ways in which people with disability are represented in popular culture texts that build upon a charity-based, individual model of

---

1 It is important to acknowledge the criticisms and limitations of the UNCRPD from a critical disability studies perspective and a Southern disability theory perspective (see Campbell, 2012; Soldatic & Grech, 2014). However, given advocacy groups' centralization of this Convention this chapter explores the potential of a rights based framing in this context.

disability. Of most relevance to an analysis of Swift is the second common representation where people with disability are represented as sweet, young, innocent beings whose disability is intended to inspire tears. Comedian and disability advocate, the late Stella Young, problematizes notions of pity and bravery, suggesting that they are "based on an assumption that the people in [these bodies] have terrible lives, and that it takes some extra kind of pluck or courage to live them" (2012). Such bodies also serve as essentially 'inspiration' and 'feel-good-tools' for able-bodied people. This is similar to arguments made by Shakespeare (2006) about the objectification of people with disability by charities used to invoke sympathy and pity by able-bodied people who feel empowered and generous by any forthcoming donations.

Shakespeare (2006) argues that tragic, sympathy inspiring or pitiful representations are problematic because it reminds the able-bodied of their capacity for goodness in a materialistic world and that they are 'fortunate' not to be like 'them' thereby serving the hegemony of ableism. What is missing from these representations are "readings of the disabled body presenting life with an impairment as an animating, affirmative modality of subjectivity" (Campbell, 2008, p. 154). Instead, the disabled body constitutes a secondary position where "non-impaired individuals and groups have relative power, while those with impairment are relatively powerless" (Thomas, 2004, p. 29). Thomas (2004) suggests that the micro and macro social relations which perpetuate the subordinated position of people with disability needs to be questioned.

In this regard, celebrity and 'pop activism' also perpetuate problematic representations of disability. McKay suggests that "disability campaigning in the mid-twentieth century set a template for much of the recent and current pop activism" (2013, p. 153) and though some of these campaigns had their limits in terms of promoting a charity perspective of disability, in other examples there is "[c]learly…a showbiz imperative, …alongside a commercial pragmatic" (p. 176) benefit at stake in reinforcing and continuing representations of people with disability as cases of charity and pity. Drawing attention to such commercial gains made on the basis of perpetuating 'tragic' representations begins to destabilize the exploitation of people with disability that occurs through celebrity charity. This type of engagement between people with disability and various public figures has been referred to by Goggin and Newell in the context of the political sphere where people with disability are instrumentalized for political gain as "the selected citizens with disabilities are wheeled out; [and] the photo opportunity begins" (2005, p. 17). As this quote demonstrates publicity and celebrity interactions are not passive, neutral or accidental, rather the interactions are positioned within wider discourses about 'normal' and 'abnormal' bodies and whose bodies deserve charitable treatment and pity, both of which comes at the expense of having equal rights. Such discourses, which underpin public relations driven interactions, also operate in the context of fan meet and greets.

Fan Meet and Greets

The fan meet and greet is a problematic interaction for achieving structural change and rights for people with disability. This is because the fan meet and greet generates attention for the celebrity rather than focusing on changing the agenda, and the power relations which operate in this context. This is because what operates in this context is what van Krieken refers to as the "vertical and asymmetrical relationship between celebrities and their audiences… [where celebrities become] super-rich in their possession of recognition capital" (2012, p. 9). Celebrities are recognized by more people than they can recognize back, and generate attention and interest beyond that afforded to the fan they are meeting, except for on the basis of their impairment. In the case of Taylor Swift's meetings with fans with disability, Swift's celebrity status eclipses the fan with disability making the interaction about Swift's generosity in meeting a fan with an impairment, rather than challenging broader hierarchies and structural inequalities experienced by people with disability. This means the human rights of people with disability as grounded in the 'DisCo' fail to be recognized through the interaction as impairment is instrumentalized and Swift maintains her image as a 'generous' celebrity.

By focusing on an individual or a small group of people in the fan meet and greet it is the existence of impairment as a barrier to a 'normal' life that becomes the driving reason for meeting the celebrity. This is a depoliticization of the wider social processes impacting on the individual or group with an impairment. A broader focus on structural barriers and the need for their eradication, according to those who support the social model, would enable the participation and inclusion of people with disability in society. However, the meet and greet interaction is forged in the objectification of impairment and does not seek to challenge social barriers. As the interaction is organized around the narrative of lamentable impairment, it means that there is often the perpetuation of a personal tragedy perspective of disability or seeing people with disability as objects of charity and pity rather than an emphasis on people with disability as being rights bearers. This interaction therefore, perpetuates the asymmetrical power relations between ability and disability. For example, in Swift's Australian '1989' tour she met several Australian fans, including a young fan with an inner ear impairment. The fan's interest and circumstance were brought to Swift's attention following local campaigns and popular pressure to arrange a meeting with Swift. Multiple newspapers focused on the impending tragedy of the young fan's hearing loss alongside the joy that the fan received in meeting Swift and attending the concert in Sydney (billed as her last chance to hear Swift sing in concert) (Brown, 2015; Iasimone, 2015). The fan's 'dreams were made true', as the fan enjoyed a moment of celebrity, overcoming 'tragic' impairment and individual circumstance. This representation foregrounds the personal tragedy of hearing loss for the fan and the charity and generosity of Swift.

Whilst perhaps not deliberate, Swift's interaction with the fans during these meetings perpetuates the individual model of disability. This is because while Swift may have the intention of subverting her status in the momentary meeting, the meeting is set within wider social relations of ability and disability, and celebrity-fan engagements. Both of which constitute a power hierarchy that privileges the celebrity in relation to the fan. Swift's meetings frame the fan's problems as stemming from the functional limitation, which arises from impairment. This representation obscures the gains the celebrity receives through this campaigning and interaction. As MacKay (2013) has suggested with regards to the commercial pragmatic of celebrities, Swift benefits commercially by reinforcing her 'generous and charitable' image through the experience of meeting fans with impairments. As such, "the non-normative body is 'created' and then... 'exploited'" (Richardson, 2012, p. 2). This occurs as the story frames the interaction as one in which the disproportionate gain is had by the person with disability at the expense of the person who is able-bodied – even if Swift were to counter that she is 'the lucky one'. This plays into wider assumptions that the able-bodied person is not "gaining as much from the relationship as the person with the disability" (Shakespeare, 2006, p. 178). Therefore, while Swift's acts do create awareness of disability and give joy to individual fans, the representations of disability that are constructed go against the lens of a human rights framing and perpetuate the dominance of ableism. As such, the fan is constituted within a discourse of pity but considered 'lucky' and deserving of charitable celebrity attention, in this instance, rather than being seen as a human being with human rights. Obscured then is the limited structural benefit this interaction generates for realizing inherent human rights for people with disability.

Shake It Off and Individualization

The focus on the individual rather than on structural mechanisms of redress is also found in Swift's own devices for dealing with media scrutiny and criticism. Swift actively manages the media and public interventions into her life to maintain her wellbeing. Conscious of her image and how she is represented, Swift does not want to be described as a *"train wreck,* [a] *mess,* [and] *terrible"*

(Raab, 2014, emphasis in original). As a "bundle… of attention capital" (van Krieken, 2012, p. 11) then, she manages her 'self'. Her music is a means for engaging with criticism whilst not being overwhelmed by the pressures of maintaining celebrity. For example, Swift identifies songs such as 'Shake it Off' as a strategy to ensure she does not "lose …[her] mind" (Swift, 2014) in response to negative comments made about her and as a mechanism to "deal with" (Kreps, 2014) the dissection and scrutinization of her life under the media gaze. She states:

> I've had every part of my life dissected – my choices, my actions, my words, my body, my style, my music … When you live your life under that kind of scrutiny, you either let it break you or you can get really good at dodging punches. And when one lands you know how to deal with it. And I guess the way I deal with it is to shake it off. (2014)

This establishes for Swift an individual coping mechanism to deal with eroded autonomy and unwanted incursions into her life. Swift shares this with her fans through the lyrics of 'Shake It Off'.

'Shake It Off' has had resonance as a tool for dealing with criticism for organizations representing people with disability and individuals with disability.[2] In fact, fan engagements with 'Shake It Off' represent disability as a positive experience and reaffirm the abilities and capacities of people with disability. These representations are largely consistent with the affirmation model of disability. For example, the song has been used by Dayna Dobias who has cerebral palsy to challenge the 'haters' who ridicule her walking. She states at the beginning of her YouTube clip:

> This is for all you haters out there. Yes, maybe my walking is weird to you and it's a little bit different than yours but I've learned to embrace it as at least when I'm walking I shake it off. (2014)

Consequently, YouTube becomes a medium to communicate alternative messages about disability from the fans once considered outside the media industry as producers of media content. A narrative which has not been colonized, devastated and told by others (Ellis, 2010) confronts Otherness and transforms the relations of who listens, who speaks and who has ownership over representations of disability (2010).

Online spaces provide a mechanism for groups previously marginalized from the production and consumption cycle to present an alternative representation (Ellis, 2016). However, for people with disability who may value the messages

---

2 See for example, Epic Arts Cambodia (2016) and Handi-Capable ShakeItOff4CP (2015).

in Swift's songs as individual coping mechanisms, the songs do not challenge the structural barriers and norms experienced by people with disability nor the incursions into their lives. For example, some people with disability lack privacy and have their rights to bodily integrity violated through forced sterilization, forced medicalization and are prohibited from other family rights (PWDA, 2010-2016). The particular human rights violations experienced by people with disability cannot be simply 'shaken off'. Therefore, a wider structural approach offered through foregrounding human rights is central to challenging disabling narratives around individualized impairment.

'Shake it Off' also assumes an attitudinal change. It requires the individual, including Swift herself, to 'shake off' concerns or criticisms. However, shaking it off again falls short as it is an individualized strategy for redress, focusing on the individual as the 'problem' or the solution and does not adequately draw attention to the wider social structure that compounds these violations for people with disability or draw attention to the discrimination and stigmatization inherent in normalizing discourses that inform social structures. Therefore, Swift's strategy does not call into question wider social structures, which privilege able-bodies and minds and generate disability as opposed to impairment. As Stella Young (2014) stated in relation to the quote, 'the only disability in life is a bad attitude':

> ...the reason that's bullshit is ... No amount of smiling at a flight of stairs has ever made it turn into a ramp. No amount of standing in the middle of bookshelf radiating a positive attitude is going to turn all those books into braille. (2014)

Young's quote demonstrates the limitations of individual attitudinal change and how this does not translate into broader structural reform without a commitment to transformation.

Conclusion

It remains that the celebrity vehicle for brand promotion in the form of meet and greets is not well situated to engage in equal human rights for people with disability. In the case of fan meet and greets the inequitable social architecture that gives rise to these conditions is one in which the message produced – even accidentally – is one of individual tragedy and not of broader social change. As such, it is important to be mindful of this when considering how 'generous' and 'charitable' celebrities are maintaining, perhaps unintentionally, existing power relations. It is for these reasons that we recommend that Swift (and perhaps other celebrities) move away from publicity generating fan meet and greets because of their capacity to instrumentalize impairment, promote the celebrity and individualize the nature of disability. Furthermore, Swift could demonstrate a commitment to structural change for people with disability by establishing a relationship with a disability advocacy organization and allowing the voices of people with disability to be heard in relation to her brand direction.

Acknowledgments

We wish to acknowledge the support and suggestions of the University of Notre Dame Australia's Arts and Sciences Writing Group in particular, Dr Christine deMatos whose comments on earlier drafts of this chapter were extremely useful. We also wish to thank the anonymous reviewers for their comments and feedback and the editors, Dr Jackie Raphael and Dr Celia Lam for their unwavering support in this process.

References

Brown, J. (2015, November 29). Taylor Swift met Jorja Hope in a fairy tale moment for the Maitland girl. *Maitland Mercury*. Retrieved from http://www.maitlandmercury.com.au/story/3525096/jorjas-wildest-dream-comes-true-when-she-meets-taylor-swift-photos/.

Campbell, F. A. K. (2008). Exploring internalized ableism using critical race theory. *Disability & Society, 23*(2), 151-162.

Campbell, F. A. K. (2012) Stalking Ableism. In D. Goodley, B. Hughes & L. J. Davis (Eds.), *Disability and social theory: New developments and directions* (pp. 212-230). Great Britain: Springer Nature.

Davis, J. (2015, December 3). Taylor Swift's Big Heart Lands Her Top Spot on Celebs Gone Good List—Again!. *In Style*. Retrieved from http://www.instyle.com/news/taylor-swift-celebs-gone-good-2015-list.

Disability Advocacy Resource Unit. (2016). *What is Disability Advocacy?* Retrieved from http://www.daru.org.au/what-is-advocacy.

Dobias, D. (2014). I "Shake It Off" When I Walk. *YouTube*. Message posted to https://www.youtube.com/watch?v=WsM0lDkyu_4.

Ellis, K. (2010). A purposeful rebuilding: Youtube, representation, accessibility and the socio-political space of disability. *Telecommunications Journal of Australia, 60*(2), 21.1 – 21.12.

Ellis, K. (2016). *Disability and Popular Culture: Focusing Passion, Creating Community and Expressing Defiance*. Oxon, New York: Routledge.

Epic Arts Cambodia. (2016). Taylor Swift – Shake It Off (Parody) by Epic Arts Cambodia. *YouTube*. Message posted to https://www.youtube.com/watch?v=wU5XWNuV4vs.

Goggin, G., & Newell, C. J. (2005). *Disability in Australia: Exposing a social apartheid.* Sydney: UNSW Press.

Handi-Capable ShakeItOff4CP. (2015). Shake It Off 4 C P. *YouTube.* Message posted to https://www.youtube.com/watch?v=spKpPrMe12Y.

Humpage, L. (2007). Models of Disability, Work and Welfare in Australia. *Social Policy and Administration, 41*(3), 215-231.

Kayess, R., & Fogarty, B. (2007). The rights and dignity of persons with disabilities: A United Nations Convention. *Alternative Law Journal, 32*(1), 22-60.

Kayess, R., & French, P. (2008). Out of darkness into light? Introducing the convention on the rights of persons with disabilities. *Human Rights Law Review, 8*(1), 1-34.

Kreps, D. (2014, August 18). Taylor Swift Dismisses the Haters, Dances with fans for new song 'Shake it Off' *Rolling Stone.* Retrieved from http://www.rollingstone.com/music/news/taylor-swift-dismisses-the-haters-dances-with-fans-for-new-song-shake-it-off-20140818.

Iasimone, A. (2015, November 29). Young Taylor Swift fan gets to meet her idol before losing hearing. *Billboard.* Retrieved from http://www.billboard.com/articles/news/6777935/taylor-swift-fan-jorja-hope-meets-idol-losing-hearing.

Look to the Stars. (2016). *Taylor Swift Charity Work, Events and Causes.* Retrieved from https://www.looktothestars.org/celebrity/taylor-swift.

McKay, G. (2013). *Shakin' all over: Popular music and disability.* Ann Arbor: University of Michigan Press.

Meekosha, H. & Shuttleworth, R. (2009). What's so 'critical' about critical disability studies? *Australian Journal of Human Rights, 15*(1), 47-75.

Oliver, M. (1996). *Understanding disability: From theory to practice.* Houndsmills, Basingstoke: Macmillan.

Oliver, M. (2013). The social model of disability. *Disability & Society, 28*(7), 1024-1026.

People with Disability Australia. (2010-2016). *Human Rights Violations.* Retrieved from, http://www.pwd.org.au/student-section/human-rights-violations.html.

People with Disability Australia. (2010-2016). *The Social Model of Disability.* Retrieved from http://www.pwd.org.au/student-section/the-social-model-of-disability.html.

Raab, S. (2014, November). Why Taylor Swift Welcomed You to New York. *Esquire.* Retrieved from http://www.esquire.com/entertainment/music/a30491/taylor-swift-1114/.

Richardson, N. (2012). *Transgressive bodies: Representations in film and popular culture*. Burlington, VT, Farnham: Ashgate Publishing.

Shakespeare, T. (2006). *Disability rights and wrongs*. New York, London: Routledge.

Soldatic, K., & Grech, S. (2014). Transnationalising Disability Studies: Rights, Justice and Impairment. *Disability Studies Quarterly*, *34*(2).

Swift, T. (2012, January 1). *First Lady Michelle Obama to Present Taylor with the Big Help Award.* Retrieved from http://taylorswift.com/news/68151.

Swift, T. (2014). *These songs were about my life. These are now about yours.* Retrieved from http://taylorswift.com/about_from_taylor.

Thomas, C. (2004). Rescuing a social relational understanding of disability. *Scandinavian Journal of Disability Research, 6*(1), 22-36.

United Nations. (2006). *Convention on the Rights of Persons with Disabilities.* Retrieved from https://www.un.org/development/desa/disabilities/convention-on-the-rights-of-persons-with-disabilities/convention-on-the-rights-of-persons-with-disabilities-2.html.

van Krieken, R. (2012). *Celebrity Society.* Oxon, New York: Routledge.

Weatherby, T. (2016, December 13). Camilla Cabello, Gigi Hadid & More Send Birthday Wishes to Taylor Swift. *Billboard.* Retrieved from, http://www.billboard.com/articles/columns/pop/7624402/taylor-swift-birthday-messages.

Young, S. (2012, July 3). We're not here for your inspiration. *The Drum.* Retrieved from, http://www.abc.net.au/news/2012-07-03/young-inspiration-porn/4107006.

Young, S. (Speaker). (2014). I'm not your inspiration, thank you very much [TED Talk]. Sydney: TED.

Commercializing Conservationism: Celebrity, Sea Shepherd, and the Pop Politics of Protest

Evan Beaumont Center

Abstract. This chapter contends that Sea Shepherd Conservation Society founder Paul Watson stands as a striking example of how the collusion of social protest, activist celebrity individualism, and transnational corporations problematizes notions of communal protest that were once held dear by the activist celebrities of yesteryear. Indeed, while 21st century activist celebrities display incredibly efficacious discourses of resistance through indomitable celebrity personas, this case study points to and problematizes a shift in activism under a neoliberal domain. In this manner, this chapter utilizes Sea Shepherd's Paul Watson as a means to illuminate paradigmatic shifts and potential pitfalls that can be correlated to a type of radical celebrity individualism that has become a salient force of resistance.

Keywords: Activism, celebrity, conservationism, neoliberalism, personae

Introduction

After six years of struggling to stop Japanese whalers in the Antarctic seas, Paul Watson, the founder of the Sea Shepherd Conservation Society, pitched their activist ventures as a reality television show (Seashepherd, 2011). After several channels balked at his pitch, in 2008, Animal Planet picked it up and titled it *Whale Wars*. The show became an instant hit while simultaneously turning Paul Watson into a celebrity.

While many reality television shows are perceived merely as entertainment puffery, *Whale Wars'* numerous accolades and political effectiveness proved to be an exception. In fact, in the immediate aftermath of Sea Shepherd's (now) highly publicized protest, Japan's Fisheries Minister Michihiko Kano declared the first shutdown of whaling along the Antarctic coast (Associated Press, 2011). Although the Japanese Whaling Industry resumed whaling the following season, the early season whaling shutdowns continued as Sea Shepherd's prolific and pestering protests gained a political foothold in their plight to protect the cetaceans of Antarctic sanctuary.

This chapter argues that Sea Shepherd's protests offer an important text through which the confluence of contemporary activism and celebrity can be understood. Specifically, this chapter turns to the study of personae in order to illuminate an individualistic neoliberal activist celebrity persona in the pursuit of high-profile publicity. Ultimately, this exploration of the rhetorical construction and deployment of Watson's persona points to a 21st century shift at the intersecting domains of neoliberalism, activism, and celebrity-driven consumerism.

Activist Individualism and Rhetorical Personae

By directing attention to the rapidly increasing discourses of consumer sovereignty, scholars assert that contemporary political practices are emphatically shifting away from the power of social collectives and towards the politics of an individualized self (Banet-Weiser, 2012; Banet-Weiser & Mukherjee, 2012; Hegde, 2011). "Packaging market-driven interests as social values," asserts Radha Hegde, "neoliberalism reshuffles the meaning of public responsibility and citizenship into the language of private choices and entitlements" (2011, p. 5). When discourses of advocacy become articulated in terms of private choices and entitlements, explains Banet-Weiser, the activist in neoliberal capitalism becomes "an entrepreneur of the self" (2012, p. 37). Hearn describes this tropological shift towards individualistic activist selves as a "shift from a working self to the self as work in the form of the self brand" (2012, p. 27). In other words, in neoliberal capitalism, the labor of the activist self moves away from the labor of collective resistance towards the practice of publicity driven self branding (Banet-Weiser, 2012). Problematically, argues Wendy Brown, this nous of neoliberal individualism glamorizes the politics of the individual at the expense of collective struggle (2003). As neoliberal individualism glamorizes the activist self as a necessary form of political resistance, it takes a foothold at the intersection of activism and celebrity.

While the nexus of activism and neoliberal individualism is regularly studied from the perspective of the consumer, it also finds a stronghold in the production of celebrity activism. Organizations like the [RED] campaign, for example, offer an excellent example of the personified rugged rhetors of neoliberal activist individualism. Perennial rock-star-activist Bono has long stood as the proverbial poster child for neoliberal humanitarianism through his [RED] campaign – an activist-centric corporate branding mechanism designed to work with corporations in order to alleviate issues of poverty on the African continent (Milmo, 2006). In this manner, Bono stands as one of many examples of how the perpetuation of celebrity works to brand individual 'selves' as points of activist resistance within the politics of the neoliberal marketplace.

In order to better understand the nexus of celebrity and activism in a neoliberal era, this chapter employs the study of Rhetorical personae. In 1970, while also referring to a market-based rhetoric of individualism, Edwin Black expounded upon rhetoric's textual construction of personae (1970). Through a close reading of text and context, Black contended that the rhetorical critic construes a rhetor's projected identity – the *first* persona – in direct relationship to their idealized audience – the *second* persona (1970). In the 1980s, building on Black's conception of rhetorical personae, Philip Wander added what he termed as the third persona: the audience that is negated in the discourse between the first and second personae. The *third* persona, asserted Wander, includes those "whose presence, though relevant to what is said, is negated through silence" (1984, p. 210). To illuminate this displaced audience, Wander challenged critics to probe the dialectical construction of the first and second personae and see how the discourse constrains the ability of "certain individuals and groups" to articulate their own voice (p. 216).

Of note, two of those who have taken up Wander's call are Charles Morris and Dana Cloud – via their respective *fourth* and *null* personae. Morris' fourth persona explains an audience's silence in relation to passing, and Cloud's null persona explains actualized silence on the part of the rhetor (Morris, 2002; Cloud, 1999). Yet, each ultimately draws from the notion of silence first articulated by Wander. "The third, null, and fourth personae are all marked by silence," summarizes Brendan Kendall (2008).

> One silence is imposed and negates audiences, another is strategically enacted by audiences aware of material constraints on their speech, and another is self-censorship employed by audiences that simultaneously appear to share ideological positions with some constituencies and positions oppositional to those constituencies. (p. 63)

Ultimately, while Wander's notion of a displaced audience was crucial to the establishment of other notions of silent personae, this chapter implores a return to the third persona when studying the activist celebrity persona.

In addition to Rhetorical Studies research, P. David Marshall, Christopher Moore, and Kim Barbour—in their expansive exposition of persona in relation to celebrity—suggest that celebrity persona should be interrogated as "material forms of public selfhood" (Marshall, Moore, & Barbour, 2015, p. 290). In this manner, they offer that these material forms of celebrity selfhood can be understood through the contexts of the celebrity position, as the celebrity negotiates through larger cultural institutions (p. 290). As this chapter asserts, Watson constructs and displays an activist celebrity persona as individualist publicity for global consumption and a form of social resistance.

Returning to Wander, the celebration of the activist celebrity persona suggests a drive towards self-branded publicity on a global scale. Watson deploys his mythological persona of an activist hero, where he is enjoined by the corporate forces of Fortune 100 Discovery Inc. (of which Animal Planet is a subsidiary) and his Sea Shepherd Conservation Society as they tap into a publicity-centric audience. This audience primarily consists of *Whale Wars* viewership and various news media outlets. Likewise, the discourse between Watson and his publicity directed audience relegates the collective activist labor of his Sea Shepherd crew to consumable fodder for publicity driven resistance. Therefore, by exploring the textual construction of Watson's aggrandized persona alongside his publicity driven audience, this chapter contends that the neoliberal activist celebrity persona deploys an entrepreneurially individualist activist self (the first persona) that procures publicity (the second persona) at the cost of silenced activist collectives (the third persona).

The Activist Celebrity Persona of Paul Watson

Paul Watson's radical and highly publicized activist pursuits have helped shape him into an activist celebrity star. Although celebrities such as Angelina Jolie, Bill Gates, Brad Pitt, Desmond Tutu, and George Clooney have used their fame to bolster activist causes, Paul Watson's celebrity differs in that it is derived solely from his activism. "Paul Watson is," affirms *The Telegraph*, "the nearest thing the environmental movement has to an action hero" (2010). Accordingly, he has strategically maneuvered his celebrity into books, movies, and endorsements by some of Hollywood's most notable A-list stars (2010). Watson intentionally keeps "celebrities actively visible, while also containing their power within the frame of the entertainment industry," states Libby Lester in a study on Sea Shepherd's publicity (2011, p. 159). Indeed, in a world of celebrity activists, Paul Watson is arguably the world's foremost activist celebrity.

Aihwa Ong asserts that in the 1970s, at the start of a rhetorical turn to neoliberal capitalism, the Horatio Alger story of the industrial revolution began to be redeployed. She states that this "rags-to-riches" story – defined by a sense of "masculine entitlement" that is paired with the assumption that "American can-do optimism, ingenuity, and hard work" will inevitably produce social success produced a narrative where "smart students tinkering in garages" could "launch a thousand computer companies" (Ong, 2006, p. 159). Interestingly, alongside the re-circulation of the Alger's narrative, came the activist organization Greenpeace. According to Margret Scammell, Greenpeace was amongst the first to hold "individual companies" responsible by "naming and shaming them for acts of environmental destruction and reckless cruelty" (2010, p. 353). Likewise, Watson's activist individualist persona – in both *Whale Wars* and his *New York Times* synopsis by award winning journalist Raffi Khatchadourian – draws heavily from his relationship with Greenpeace. His mythic ethos is deeply invested in his foundational role in the organization and his entrepreneurial spirit is especially advanced through their split. As Raffi Khatchadourian points out, Watson is deft in his construction of an "indomitable persona" (2007). Likewise, Khatchadourian's *New Yorker* profile of Sea Shepherd Watson's persona reflects a quintessential narrative of Horatio Algers-esaue neoliberal activist individualism – a persona that is only accentuated by a tumultuous relationship with Greenpeace.

The persona of Paul Watson includes an enumeration of tall tales and exaggerated anecdotes. In "mixing propaganda with action," Khatchadourian asserts, "Watson has a habit of blending fact with rhetoric" and "through embellishment, he used his adventures to construct an indomitable persona" (2007). In his early beginnings these mythic contours included his early onset environmental radical status as an "eco-warrior before puberty" (2007), who overcame an abusive father to find himself as a homeless college student caught up in radical environmental movements in the 1960s. Subsequently, he joined the merchant marines and had a number of nearly unbelievable adventures such as witnessing live bombings in Vietnam; reading Conrad's Typhoon while in an actual typhoon; and being tortured by Shah security agents in Iran. When Watson describes his background, asserts Khatchadourian, he seems "unable to discuss his personal history without giving it mythic contours," possessing what "George Orwell once called a 'lonely child's habit of making up stories'" (2007).

It is no coincidence that the Horatio Algers 'pick yourself up by your bootstraps' narrative of neoliberal individualism is especially apparent through his relationship with Greenpeace. Without unraveling Greenpeace's claims to the contrary, Khatchadourian asserts that Watson was among "some two dozen other environmental activists" who helped create Greenpeace (2007). Indeed, Watson regularly draws upon this story in interviews by referring to a life changing moment that he has retold "countless times" (2007). This story frames Watson as a rogue member of a young Greenpeace who encouraged another member to break from their collective group in order to confront a gargantuan Soviet whaling fleet in a tiny zodiac. Upon their arrival, they watched as a harpoon whizzed above their heads and sank into the flesh of a sperm whale. The injured whale reacted by charging towards their tiny zodiac. Yet, immediately before destroying the men and their boat, the dying sperm whale supposedly made eye contact, expressed a sense of compassionate recognition, and succinctly stopped in its proverbial tracks – they "were overcome with emotion" (Khatchadourian, 2007).

Although Watson's foundational relationship with Greenpeace is an important part of his persona, their amicable relationship was short lived. Despite the fact that Watson's whale encounter "generated widespread publicity and donations" (Lester, 2011, p. 127), he was expelled from the organization less than two years after the encounter. The reason he was ousted, explained Khatchadourian, was ultimately due to an aggressive response to an anti-sealing protest in Canada. This was the tipping point for Greenpeace. The organization with nonviolence in their namesake decided that they could no longer tolerate Watson's aggressive actions. "Many board members believed that Watson's actions violated the group's pacifist ethos", explained Khatchadourian (2007). Among those who voted him out was Robert Hunter, a journalist who is often described as Greenpeace's most influential member. "[I]n terms of the Greenpeace gestalt," remarked Hunter, "he seemed possessed by…a desire to push himself front and center, shouldering everyone else aside" (Khatchadourian, 2007). In sum, Watson's extreme and oftentimes violent actions – especially when paired with a growing sense of egotism – were too much for Greenpeace to stomach.

Concomitant with his ever-growing celebrity status, in 2008, Watson became the force behind the hit Emmy-nominated show *Whale Wars*. He was the one who initially pitched the show to Animal Planet and he plays a huge part in both the production and publicity of Sea Shepherd's activism (Strauss, 2008). Concerning production, as each whaling season begins, the Sea Shepherd crew sets sail in the Antarctic seas and Animal Planet provides an onboard camera crew who records, edits, and uploads footage (Khatchadourian, 2013). *Whale Wars* is then produced and broadcast the next summer as a collaborative effort; their actions are primarily strategized by Capitan Paul Watson and then edited and produced for the silver screen by Animal Planet. "We would not direct in any way what the Sea Shepherds would do," avows senior vice president of legal and business affairs Julie Wolf (Dehnart, 2013). The final product, as described by Animal Planet Presided Majorie Kaplan, is a "character-based adventure drama set in one of the most magnificent places on Earth – like 'Deadliest Catch' meets 'Moby-Dick" (Kaufman, 2010). Likewise, the drama of *Whale Wars* provides Watson a stage upon which he can star.

From the start of *Whale Wars*, Watson's activist celebrity persona is immediately framed as central to the show. As the very first episode opens the voice of the narrator frames each show via a short biography of Watson. Watson is described as a "legend in the environmental movement" and as one who "cofounded Greenpeace" (Bronstein, 2008a). In a true Horatio Alger-like spirit of rugged individualism the narrator reminds the audience that "[Watson] started his own organization, Sea Shepherd, and he makes his own rules" (Bronstein, 2008a). These proclamations are set to a scenic backdrop that portrays Watson as a rugged, adventure-seeking and nature-loving hero of the Antarctic, which is buttressed by photos that show him cuddling with baby seals and other cute Antarctic creatures (Bronstein, 2008a; Bronstein, 2008b). Even the oft-condemning *Wall Street Journal* describes Animal Planet's narrative of

Watson as a "hagiography, with rock music to underscore praise for 'the legend in the environmental movement,'" adding that Watson is portrayed as one of "compassionate wrath" who "will die for the whales" (Smith, 2008). As Watson stars in *Whale Wars,* his perpetual drive for publicity is ever on display.

Amidst the filming and production of *Whale Wars*, Watson works extensively with news media in order to gain the most publicity for his activist endeavors. "We live in a media culture – the camera is probably the most powerful weapon we have in the world," states Watson in the second episode of *Whale Wars* (Bronstein, 2008b). Accordingly, Lester states that media outlets "commonly reflect Watson's preferred frames, use images supplied by Sea Shepherd, and/or prominently quote Watson and his spokespeople" (2011, p. 125). For instance, while filming *Whale Wars*, Watson and Animal Planet work together to produce real-time publicity that leads up to the airing of each season (2011).

This process is apparent from the get go. In the initial episodes, under the pretext of protest, *Whale Wars'* plot is derived from Watson's scheme to illegally sneak Sea Shepherd volunteers onboard a Japanese whaling ship in the hopes that they will force an international hostage situation. After pestering the whaling ship enough to distract its crew, Sea Shepherd gets two of its own crewmembers aboard, risking a fatal fall into the icy Antarctic waters. Once aboard, Watson excitedly proclaims, "The longer we can keep them on that boat, the better the story [will] be!" (Bronstein, 2008b). The cameras then cut to Sea Shepherd First Mate Peter Brown, who jovially echoes Watson's sentiment, "If we can keep the incident in the newspapers, and on the news, maybe the Japanese government will decide it's time to pack it in!" (Bronstein, 2008b). Watson's jubilation is palpable as he perpetuates the drama in pursuit of publicity.

Immediately after this 'hostage situation' the episode portrays the news publicity process. With Watson leading the way, photos and videos are immediately forwarded to the press. Urgently Watson asks, "Did we get any good still photographs of them up there too? Because that's a picture that's going to go around the world – [so] get that picture!" (Bronstein, 2008b). Afterwards, Watson carefully chooses a photo of one of the new hostages screaming and releases it to the media. Once Watson releases these photos, albeit with his spin, news media jump on the story. Omitting Animal Planet's help, the narrator's voice cuts over images of Sea Shepherd's press scramble. "Within hours of informing the press of the hostage situation, the story breaks worldwide," explains the narrator. Accordingly, it is Watson who receives the credit for his crew's protests (Bronstein, 2008b).

Watson's leadership and sense of rugged individualism is regularly juxtaposed against his supporting crew – a collective batch of volunteer activists who are oftentimes portrayed as incompetent neophytes and expendable pawns in Watson's battle to save the earth. "[T]he dramatic tension [of *Whale Wars*] comes mainly from watching his amateurish, incompetent, bickering crew make an incredible, agonizing series of blunders," describes *The Telegraph*. "You watch it on the edge of your seat, shaking your head and clasping it from time to time, waiting to see what will go wrong next and if it will get someone killed" (Paul Watson, 2010). DeWolf Smith of *The Wall Street Journal* adds that the "unseemly glee that random crewmembers display about this chance to play hero and, thanks to the Japanese and the whales, give some excitement and meaning to their otherwise mundane lives." Bitingly she asserts that, "Although the word 'deadly' is used often to underscore the risks the crew face, alone out in the wild Antarctic seas – their own incompetence can seem the most frightening" (Smith, 2008). Similarly, throughout the series Watson regularly sits in relative safety as he risks the lives of his haphazard and ill-trained crew.

Much like his days with Greenpeace, it is Watson that stands at the forefront of the narrative frames of radical conservationism. Likewise, it is Watson that gets the credit for his crew's risky maneuvers. Clips from Australian, American, British, and Japanese news reporting on the situation are shown and the scene moves on. "People say I manipulate the media…Well, duh," reveals Watson in an interview. "We live in a media culture so why on earth wouldn't I?" he adds:

> What we do is provide the media with the kind of stories they can't resist, even if they really try, and this is how we bring attention to what's happening to the whales, the seals, the sharks and the other marine conservation campaigns we're involved in. (The Telegraph, 2010)

Thus, in the process of building an aggrandized activist celebrity persona, those who provide material support for him are regularly displaced. In fact, Watson's tumultuous relationship with Greenpeace still plays out on the public stage. On *Whale Wars*, this relationship is made evident when Sea Shepherd radios them for help locating Japanese whaling ship. Illustrating the divide between the two organizations, Sea Shepherd calls Greenpeace, requests help, and can then barely finish an exchange before Greenpeace hangs up on them.

Unsurprisingly, with a particular focus on Watson, Greenpeace has publicly responded to Sea Shepherd's divisive accusations. For instance, they have dedicated a section of their official website in order to defend Watson's claims against them. After countering Sea Shepherd's claims that Greenpeace does little more than "film whales being killed" the website concludes. "Paul Watson is welcome to express his opinions about Greenpeace – as a radical environmental organization, we have a wide spectrum of detractors, and we welcome fair criticism," they explain. "But, we expect fair debate to be based in fact, not falsehoods" (Greenpeace, 2016). Ultimately, Watson's individualism bleeds through Sea Shepherd as he continues to obfuscate the efforts of those, like Greenpeace, who offer conservationist resistance for the same ends.

Conclusion

As consumerism continues to exude a phenomenological force for transnational politics one cannot ignore the importance of the celebrities as they endorse the commodified products of social justice. However, when Watson stands as a self-made activist in the vein of neoliberalism, one must wonder what the larger ramifications of activist celebrity individualism may be. Indeed, in the vein of a hegemonic Horatio Algers narrative that justifies privilege and success as the mere products of individualistic agency, scholars of both celebrity and resistance must problematize stories of white male activist heroes, who activate protest, but can neutralize the threat of collective resistance by overshadowing the plight of their colleagues, supporters, and founding organizations. Indeed, Watson's neoliberal activist celebrity persona celebrates individualism while simultaneously displacing those that have made his ascent to stardom possible.

Acknowledgments

Evan Beaumont Center, PhD would like to thank his partner, Sabrina – as this paper came out of our honeymoon. He would also like to thank Christopher Newport University for funding the grant that made this research possible.

References

Banet-Weiser, S. (2012). *Authentic TM: Politics and ambivalence in a brand culture.* New York, NY: New York University Press.

Banet-Weiser, S. & Mukherjee, R. (2012). Introduction: Commodity Activism in Neoliberal Times. In R. Mukherjee & S. Banet-Weiser (Eds.), *Commodity activism: Cultural resistance in neoliberal times* (pp. 23-38). New York, NY: New York University Press.

Black, E. (1970). The second persona. *Quarterly Journal of Speech, 56* (2), 109-119.

Bronstein, B. (Producer). (2008a). Season One Episode One: Needle in a Haystack [Television Broadcast]. In B. Bronstein (Producer), *Whale Wars*. Silver Spring, MD: Animal Planet.

Bronstein, B. (Producer). (2008b). Season One Episode Two: Nothing's Ideal [Television Broadcast]. In B. Bronstein (Producer), *Whale Wars.* Silver Spring, MD: Animal Planet.

Brown, W. (2003). Neo-liberalism and the End of Liberal Democracy. *Theory & Event,* 7(1), Retrieved from https://muse.jhu.edu/article/48659.

Cloud, D. (1999). The null persona: Race and the rhetoric of silence in the uprising of '34. *Rhetoric & Public Affairs,* 2(2), 177-209.

Dehnart, A. (2013). Not their whale war anymore: How animal planet was forced to step down. The *Wire.* Retrieved from http://www.thewire.com/entertainment/2013/12/not-their-whale-war-anymore-how-animal-planet-was-forced-step-down/356026.

Greenpeace. (2016). *Paul Watson, Sea Shepherd and Greenpeace: Some Facts.* Retrieved from http://www.greenpeace.org/international/en/about/history/paul-watson/.

Hearn, A. (2012). Brand Me "Activist." In R. Mukherjee & S. Banet-Weiser (Eds.), *Commodity activism: Cultural resistance in neoliberal times* (pp. 23-38). New York, NY: New York University Press.

Hegde, R. S. (2011). *Circuits of visibility: Gender and transnational media cultures.* New York, NY: New York University Press.

Japan Ends Whaling Season Early. (2011, February 17). *Associated Press.* Retrieved from http://today.msnbc.msn.com/id/41656257/ns/world_news-world_environment.

Kaufman, A. (2010, June 4). 'Whale Wars' capital Paul Watson swims with the pod. *Los Angeles Times.* Retrieved from http://articles.latimes.com/2010/jun/04/entertainment/la-et-whalewars-20100604.

Kendall, B. (2008). Personae and natural capitalism: Negotiating politics and constituencies in a rhetoric of sustainability. *Environmental Communication,* 2(1), 59-77.

Khatchadourian, R. (2007, May 11). Neptune's Navy. *The New Yorker.* Retrieved from http://www.newyorker.com/reporting/2007/11/05/071105fa_fact_khatchadourian.

Khatchadourian, R. (2013, June 4). Whale-war fugitive: Q&A with Paul Watson. *The New Yorker.* Retrieved from http://www.newyorker.com/online/blogs/newsdesk/2013/06/whale-war-fugitive-q-a-with-paul-watson.html.

Lester, L. (2011). Species of the month: Anti-whaling, mediated visibility, and the news. *Environmental Communication: A Journal of Nature and Culture.* 5(1), 124-139.

Marshall, P. D., Moore, C., & Barbour, K. (2015). Persona as method: Exploring celebrity and the public self through persona studies. *Celebrity Studies, 6*(3), 288-305.

Milmo, C. (2006, January 27). Ethical Shopping: The RED Revolution. *The Belfast Telegraph.* Retrieved from http://www.belfasttelegraph.co.uk/imported/ethical-shopping-the-red-revolution-28252943.html.

Morris, C. E. (2002). Pink herring & the fourth persona: J. Edgar Hoover's sex crime panic. *Quarterly Journal of Speech, 88*(2), 228-244.

Ong, A. (2006). *Neoliberalism as exception: Mutations in citizenship and sovereignty.* Durham, NC: Duke University Press.

Paul Watson: Sea Shepherd Eco-Warrior Fighting to Stop Whaling and Seal Hunts. (2010). *The Telegraph.* Retrieved from http://www.telegraph.co.uk/earth/5166346/Paul-Watson-Sea-Shepherd-eco-warrior-fighting-to-stop-whaling-and-seal-hunts.html.

Scammell, M. (2010). The internet and civic engagement: The age of the citizen-consumer. *Political Communication, 17*(4), 351-355.

Seashepherd. (2011). *The History of Sea Shepherd.* Retrieved from http://www.seashepherd.org/who-we-are/our-history.html.

Smith, N. D. (2008, November 7). Surprising Adventures. *The Wall Street Journal,* W9C.

Strauss, G. (2008, November 7). 'Whale' saviors on warpath: Series' team chases Japanese hunters. *USA Today,* 15D.

Wander, P. (1984). The third persona: An ideological turn in rhetorical theory. *Central States Speech Journal,* 35, 197-216.

Part II:
Politics and Presentation

Conflicted Celebrity in Media:
Graffiti Artists and Pixadores in the Brazilian Press

Alexander Araya López

Abstract. This paper examines the social phenomena of street art (hip-hop graffiti) and pixação/pichação in Brazil, comparing the discourses associated with the producers of these practices, by analyzing news articles and opinion columns published by the newspaper *Folha de São Paulo (FSP)* between 2001 and 2010. The national and international success of Brazilian graffiti artists OsGemeos (The Twins) is compared to the controversial actions of pixadores, both in the streets and within artistic institutions in Brazil and abroad. These cases allow us to observe the differences between individual and collective forms of celebrity, and between 'positive' and 'negative' media representations of the graffiti artists and pixadores.

Keywords: Graffiti, media, criminology, art, urban youth

Introduction: On graffiti and the Brazilian Pixação

The study of 'graffiti' is often difficult because this term refers to a series of social phenomena with distinctive causes and cultural contexts. 'Graffiti' encompasses not only inscriptions in public bathrooms (latrinalia), but signatures and names (tagging culture), political statements (political graffiti) and finally, the more commercialized, mainstream version of urban street art (or hip-hop graffiti) (Araya López, 2015). The term, in the common usage, is frequently associated with the social imaginary of young urban teenage males (Austin, 2001; Ferrell, 1993), who wander around with spray cans leaving their marks on walls, either from 'boredom' or while pursuing an 'irrational adrenalin fix'.

The academic discussion on graffiti has separately focused on all these dissimilar phenomena, emphasizing the complexity of graffiti practices (in plural).[1] Considering this, it is necessary to challenge the popular assumptions about graffiti (in singular), confronting it with both theoretical and empirical insights related to the different practices. While it is partially true that many producers of 'graffiti' are young urban teenage males, other 'unrepresented' groups such as adults, women and/or political activists are also found among graffiti producers. Moreover, I propose to understand graffiti practices as something more than the production of an inscription or an artwork on a public

---

[1] Austin (2001), Ferrell (1993), Kozak (2004), Lachmann (1988), and Ventura (2009).

surface. Given that these inscriptions work as communicative devices, these practices presuppose an audience (or are aimed at consumers), with a message directed toward a specific group or to the general population.

As with age, the class and race of graffiti producers are diverse. Graffiti is frequently considered as a practice predominant among lower class youth, but high/middle-income producers are not necessarily rare. While historically associated with Latino and Black populations in New York, graffiti practices have spread throughout the globe and no racial group can claim ownership of these practices. While 'graffiti' is often perceived as an anonymous practice, an important number of graffiti artists are well-known individuals and have attained *celebrity status* (for example, Jean-Michel Basquiat, Keith Haring, and Banksy).

The consumption of graffiti, which has frequently been overlooked by academics, includes the observation of physical graffiti on the walls and also manifold reproductions of these creations in websites, movies (documentaries), and specialized literature (including books on graffiti, graffiti kits and DIY manuals). This market for graffiti consumption seems to be associated with the supposed coolness and rebellious nature of the practice, inspired by the marginality of its origins in New York in the 1970s.

However, the very origins of modern graffiti practices (street art and tagging culture) are unclear. While some consider New York as the rightful birthplace of tagging culture, others refute this statement by highlighting the importance of other graffiti scenes in places like Philadelphia.[2] Political graffiti and its origins are also hard to track (Kozak, 2004; Austin, 2001; Ferrell, 1993).

Similarly, while some graffiti practices are considered countercultural,[3] other graffiti productions are in synchrony with the goals of institutions and corporations. Graffiti is occasionally produced as advertising, or with means and under conditions previously approved by artistic institutions, businesses and corporations or with the patronage and support of local or governmental authorities. The emergence of tolerance zones (Austin, 2001) for graffiti production is not rare in contemporary urban environments, even when these areas could significantly curtail the lifestyle associated with graffiti practices

---

[2] Austin (2001) suggests that the writing practice did not begin in New York, but in Philadelphia, perhaps around 1959. The exact site of origin of these practices has no relevance for this analysis.

[3] Or perceived as an act of civil disobedience, following the definition by Habermas (1996).

(Araya López, 2015, p. 86; Ferrell, 1993)[4] and affect the political significance of the practice.[5] Additionally, NGOs and youth institutions have used (hip-hop) graffiti/street art to foster self-esteem and a sense of belonging among peripheral/urban youth, with the objective of minimizing the chances of their involvement with criminal organizations or (unproductive) risk behaviors (which include the 'ugly' manifestations of graffiti, i.e. tagging culture).

Indeed, graffiti practices are both welcomed and punished, fostered and censored, and the boundaries between the practices and the 'legitimate' uses of public spaces are difficult to assess. On the one hand, art institutions and museums may promote graffiti and street art, while at the same time urban planners, local authorities and police officers discourage and prosecute their producers. These clashing narratives and discourses are noticeable in both news articles and opinion columns. In principle, graffiti practices seem to be easily accepted when their nature is not perceived as a threat to the economic system of production, and/or when the aesthetics are read as an improvement or an embellishment of urban (public) spaces.

Some graffiti artists have responded to this 'social acceptance' by moving their productions from the streets to the canvas (and published books), while also creating designer products and selling their creations as interior design and advertisement. The international success of artists like Banksy has placed graffiti in the spotlight, and while the upper/middle classes consume *postgraffiti* art,[6] countercultural and disenfranchised voices within the graffiti scene denounce the cooptation of their practice and the commodification of their urban culture. 'Graffiti' is, therefore, a contested culture with contested notions of public space. It is important to distinguish this mainstream commodification of graffiti from the emergence of subcultural markets, where young producers create their own magazines, videos and products for internal consumption, and sometimes for non-economic exchange (as occurs in the subcultural world of the Brazilian pixação).

---

[4] For example, by regulating the place and time of the production, censoring specific topics or providing adult supervision of a 'youth practice'.

[5] Gonos et. al. (1976) and Stocker et. al. (1972) highlight how political graffiti reflect the social attitudes of the community, or sometimes express opinions considered 'controversial' or 'unpopular' (mostly because of its anonymous nature).

[6] *Postgraffiti* refers to stickers, posters, sculptures, mosaics, stencils, knitting and other forms of art created with materials different to 'traditional' spray paint. *Postgraffiti* also refers to graffiti art created directly on canvas, although this definition is open to debate.

The controversy about graffiti is not only evident in these official approaches to the practice, but is also visible in the discourses related to the production and consumption of graffiti inscriptions and artworks. While some people appreciate, and are open to street art, their feelings about tagging or political graffiti may be negative. While some praise graffiti as alternative urban art, other social groups highlight the criminogenic nature of 'graffiti', by comparing (selected) graffiti practices with other manifestations of urban disorder, including pollution, homelessness and prostitution. Graffiti productions are likewise perceived as an affront to an idealized sense of belonging and civility, mostly in the form of social heritage or identity (Araya López, 2015).

The Brazilian graffiti and pixação are examples of these discursive struggles. While local authorities use the word 'pichação' to refer to both political and undecipherable inscriptions on the walls, the young producers defend their 'pixação' as a countercultural movement. The pichação/pixação is an autochthonous calligraphy, expressed mostly in the form of signatures made on surfaces with black ink, which have a transgressive political nature. The pixadores, frequently identifying themselves as peripheral/disenfranchised youth, claim the urban spaces as an act of defiance against the local authorities and the citizenry in general. While 'graffiti' is welcomed and fostered by art institutions, corporations and local authorities, pixação is considered a nuisance, a criminal act and risk behavior. Indeed, there is an official graffiti day in Brazil,[7] while the authorities are always pursuing new anti-pixação strategies and campaigns.[8] Moreover, graffiti workshops have even been implemented to fight the pixadores, by turning them into (productive) entrepreneurs and artists (Francisco, 2005).

This chapter focuses on discourses regarding both the Brazilian graffiti artists and the pixadores published in the newspaper *Folha de São Paulo (FSP)* between 2001 and 2010. A sample of 682 news articles and opinion columns were reviewed for this study.[9] The search was based on the keyword *graffiti* (with the variation of *grafite* in Portuguese) and included related words such as *street art, grafiteiro/a* and *pichação-pixação* (Araya López, 2015, p. 75). Two examples have been selected for the purposes of this chapter: Firstly, in relation to the Brazilian street art, the national and international success of the brothers

---

[7] The *Dia Nacional do Grafite* is celebrated on March 27th in commemoration of the death of Alex Vaullari, considered one of its most important pioneers in Brazil (Araujo, 2010).

[8] One article mentions that the anti-pixação solution adopted by the local authorities was as bad as the problem, merely substituting "stains of pichação" for "stains of concrete". (Brito, 2005).

[9] This chapter includes more recent references for both the case of OsGemeos and the pixadores, with the object of keeping the controversy up to date.

OsGemeos will be discussed. Second, to approach the controversy related to the pichação/pixação, this chapter reviews the series of attacks organized by pixadores against art institutions and galleries in 2008, concluding with their participation in the Bienal de São Paulo in 2010.

The theoretical perspective of this research includes the discussion on the concept of publicity and the public sphere (Habermas, (1990 [1962]), following the idea of subaltern counterpublics (Fraser, 1990) and diasporic publics (Avritzer & Costa, 2004)). This approach relies on the methodology of discourse analysis proposed by Altheide (1997) who states that media texts include a 'problem' frame oriented toward the allocation of responsibility. Subaltern publics challenge the media discourses about them by creating their own alternative media, a form of *contentious pluralism* (Guidry & Sawyer, 2003). The theoretical framework includes the sociology of space and of the cities (Löw, 2001, 2010), cultural criminology (Ferrell, 1999), and critical geography on urban spaces (Harvey, 2012), among others.

The news articles and opinion columns were coded and analyzed following the qualitative methodology of discourse analysis proposed by Tonkiss (2004, p. 378), which consists of three basic steps: a) identifying key themes and arguments, b) looking for variation in time, and c) paying attention to silences. Articles were also codified accordingly to the sources included (i.e. police, scholars, graffiti artists, etc.) and by categories of graffiti practice.

OsGemeos, Supergrafiteiros and Brazilian Graffiti Art

Otávio and Gustavo Pandolfo are known worldwide as OsGemeos (The Twins), a pair of street artists originally from the traditional neighborhood of Cambuci, São Paulo. An analysis of news and opinion articles published in *FSP* shows that OsGemeos are the graffiti artists most frequently mentioned by the newspaper (Araya López, 2015, p. 208).[10] According to Franco (2009, p. 32-165), Brazilian graffiti is the outcome of the influence of the same movement in New York. Franco explains how a group of pioneers (including artists like Rui Amaral and Alex Vaullari in the 1980s) was the necessary inspiration for the emergence of the Old School of Brazilian graffiti (1990-2000). Among them, such well-known names as OsGemeos, Tinho, and Speto are characterized by the adoption of the tenets of hip-hop culture. The New School of Brazilian graffiti (from 2000 until today including artists such as Boleta, Zezão and Nigazz, as well as the pixadores) represents a rupture with hip-hop

---

[10] OsGemeos were mentioned in 49 articles. The second place was Titi Freak with 18 articles, followed by Nunca with 16.

culture, because of the exploration of new forms of expression, more abstract and collective than those of the previous generation.

In this sense, OsGemeos are a classic of Brazilian graffiti and an icon of worldwide graffiti culture. They have exhibited their work in Brazil and internationally, such as in London, Paris, Milan, Tokyo, Los Angeles, New York, Berlin, Havana, Hong Kong and Athens (Wainer, 2005). They have collaborated with Nike, launching a sneaker which they designed, and the *New York Times* newspaper published a story praising the duo and stating that their works are valued up to US$15,000 in the United States (Wainer, 2005). Moreover, OsGemeos established a record number of visitors during their exhibition at the gallery Fortes Vilaça, with 30,000 visitors in two months (Wainer, 2007).

Beyond the specialized audience that consumes graffiti productions and street art, OsGemeos seem to appeal to Brazilian society as a whole. Their status is linked not only to the merit of their work, but also to the status of the institutions that have welcomed them, for example, the Tate Modern in London (Nadin & Fioratti, 2008). To borrow a concept mentioned in one of the articles about graffiti workshops aimed at Brazilian youth, OsGemeos could be considered as *supergrafiteiros,* enjoying a status that is not comparable with the experiences of the average graffiti artist. Not only are they able to create and sell their work, enjoying both economic rewards and political influence, but they are also able to create their own 'news', for instance, by denouncing attacks against their artwork (perpetrated by pixadores or by local authorities), or by demanding recognition.

Otávio Pandolfo, referring to one of these incidents,[11] commented in an article: "It is disrespect. We paint a castle in Scotland, the city hall of New York calls us to create a work there. We are respected and known around the world. Here, in our home, we are not" (Furlaneto, 2008). While painting over such works seems to be part of the ongoing struggle against illegal/unauthorized graffiti,[12] OsGemeos consider themselves as immune to this removal (censorship). They demand that their works be recognized as something of untold artistic value, something 'sacred' (i.e. something that needs to be preserved) on the wall. After their comments denouncing the abuse against their work, OsGemeos (and their coworkers Nunca and Nina) were able to force a

---

[11] This complaint refers to the removal of a commissioned graffiti mural painted in 2002 with the support of the former Mayor Marta Suplicy.

[12] The law *Cidade Limpa* (14223) regulates a series of topics related to urban aesthetics from dumpsters to public toilets. The law allegedly contributed to the use of commissioned graffiti.

public apology by the local authorities (Nadin & Fioratti, 2008). Indeed, the city hall invited them to create another mural, in the same place where their previous work had been removed, according to the authorities, "by mistake" during a campaign against pixação (Furlaneto, 2008).

The celebrity and success of OsGemeos cannot be attributed only to the merit of their work and their unique aesthetics, but must consider current trends in the art market, the status of the institutions that have hosted them and even more subjective matters such as individual taste (of potential consumers in the Brazilian upper/middle classes and/or the advertising industry). Indeed, while OsGemeos can successfully place their art in both the streets and the museums with few restrictions, it is naïve to imagine that the majority of graffiti artists in Brazil could enjoy a similar status, with its correlated benefits in both economic and symbolic power.

The Controversial Art and Politics of Brazilian Pixação

Considered a crime and a nuisance in São Paulo and other Brazilian cities, pixação does not enjoy the acceptance that 'graffiti' has acquired. The pixadores perceive themselves as a *movement*, oriented toward both the transformation and appropriation of urban spaces through the politics of transgression. They create pixação to include themselves, by force, in the aesthetics of the city. They consider this aggression the 'natural' response to the politics of segregation, stigmatization and exclusion, produced not only by political decisions but also by the capitalist system itself (Araya López, 2015).

According to news articles and opinion columns published in *FSP*, pixação was at first linked to medical-epidemiological, legal and criminogenic discourses (Araya López, 2015, p. 123). In this sense, the pixadores were considered as a plague: animal-like individuals unable to restrain themselves and governed by irrational drives. They were compared to insects (*bichos*) and little pigs (*porcolinos*) that "need to be contained".[13] The practice of pixação not only polluted, but was read as pointless vandalism, going against the most basic notions of citizenship and heritage. Additionally, and related to the orthodox model of the Broken Windows theory (Wilson & Kelling, 1982), pixação was read as a sign of social decay, inviting more serious forms of crime by sending the message that social control is poorly enforced or not enforced at all.

---

[13] Some of the anti-pixação columns were written by Antonio Ermírio de Moraes, one of the wealthiest Brazilian billionaires. De Moraes's columns targeted not only the pichação, but other problems "caused" by pollution and homelessness (Araya López, 2015, p. 125).

These early discourses about pixação (published mostly between 2001 and 2005) do not mention any type of positive outcome related to the practice, such as, for instance, the sense of belonging among peripheral youth, the improvement in self-esteem or the exploration of artistic creativity (Araya López, 2015; following Lachmann, 1998). The inscriptions are considered devoid of political meaning, and are presented as indecipherable scribbling (Araya López, 2015, p. 126). To fight the negative publicity and discourses associated with their practice, the pixadores organized a series of 'collective attacks' against established art institutions in Brazil. The collective actions included the production of pixação on artistic works created by formal Brazilian artists, sometimes also targeting the work of established graffiti artists (including OsGemeos).

In 2008, the pixador Rafael Augustaitiz organized a collective 'violent' action as part of a (failed) graduation project from Belas Artes[14] (Capriglione, 2008a). That same year, another 'attack' took place against the gallery Choque Cultural, an institution mostly linked to graffiti art (Mercier, 2008). Pixadores were allegedly expressing their dislike of these commercialized forms of graffiti. The last collective action was the appropriation of the 'empty space' in the *28ª Bienal Internacional de Arte de São Paulo*. This 'attack' was a response to the curatorship of the Biennale, which supposedly proposed an artistic meditation on "the void" (Choque, 2008). If the space was empty, the pixadores decided to take it. The group entered the pavilion Oscar Niemeyer (protected by heritage laws) and placed their 'art' on the walls. This action was the most important of the 'attacks' organized by the pixadores, in part because it concluded with the imprisonment of the pixadora Caroline Pivetta da Mota (Muniz, 2008).

The Caroline case attracted a great deal of attention and became a public debate. After Ms. Pivetta da Mota was detained for not having a legal address, her arrest was called into question by academic, artistic and even political authorities (Araya López, 2015, p. 138-139). Caroline was allegedly the only female pixadora who took part in the attack, and her imprisonment was considered 'politically-motivated', 'gender-biased' and 'excessive' (Capriglione, 2008b).

After this event, pixadores started to enjoy a period of controversial social recognition. The documentary *Pixo* (Wainer & Oliveria, 2009), locally produced with the participation of the pixadores, became particularly important because it presented the practice from the perspective of its creators. In 2010,

---

[14] The Centro Universitário de Belas Artes de São Paulo is a private institution for the study of arts and design.

following the violent collective actions experienced at the previous Biennale, the pixadores were invited to take part in the exposition (Mena, 2010), but even this invitation was not enough to avoid all potential controversy. During their participation, the pixadores were still able to create another 'artistic scandal' by attacking an artwork, which included "vultures in captivity" (Vaz & Martí, 2010), demanding their liberation.[15]

This success of the pixadores in placing their movement and transgressive art inside official art institutions was not only an outcome of the 'attacks', but also a response to the internationalization of pixação. In 2009, a small group of pixadores was invited to 'decorate' the walls of the *Fondation Cartier* in Paris, as part of the exhibition 'Né dans la rue – Graffiti' (Born in the streets). Their participation included the screening of the documentary *Pixo*. This international recognition of pixação was important for the subsequent celebrity of the pixadores, who were not only included in the next edition of the São Paulo Biennale, but were also invited to other international events such as the 2012 Biennale in Berlin. As is typical of this practice and its producers, another conflict emerged out of the power struggle between the transgressive nature of the pixadores and the rules given to them by the curatorship of the Berlin Biennale (Wainer, 2012). The pixadores refused to create their work in the designated area and expanded their art to unauthorized surfaces inside a church protected by heritage laws.[16]

A series of new events, which require further analysis, illustrates the evolution of the pixação movement. A new film, *Pixadores* (Escandari, 2014), has been produced, showing the origins and daily life of the pixadores, regarding their participation in the Berlin Biennale. In 2015, two pixadores were also killed by the police in a controversial encounter inside an apartment building. While the families and friends maintain that they were executed and that the sole interest of the 'victims' was in doing pixação, the police insist that the two men were 'robbers' caught in the act, resisting arrest (Martins & Naísa, 2014).

It is worth mentioning that even though pixadores and their practice have achieved some national and international recognition and pixação is now socially perceived as an artistic practice by a small sector of the population, the legislation against pixação is clear and severe. The practice is considered a

---

[15] The pichador demanded the liberation of the vultures after a local NGO protested the Biennale, drawing attention to the conditions in which the animals were kept (Vaz & Martí, 2010).

[16] This case was reported in both Brazilian and German press in 2012, however this research only concerns media texts from 2001 to 2010.

criminal activity, punished by fines and jail terms. In the news articles analyzed for this research, a series of articles mentioned efforts taken by local authorities to promote graffiti art as a way to prevent the "harmful and dangerous" practice of pixação (Pinheiro, 2001). Pixação is not only perceived as a threat to others (i.e. with physical victims such as property owners and citizens or symbolic victims such as 'the heritage'), but also as a threat to the pixadores themselves. The self-victimization is evident not only because of the legal consequences of their actions, but because pixadores are frequently injured or killed while pursuing this activity.

The celebrity of a pixador, however, is linked not only to the risks taken in order to produce a given inscription (for example, higher sites grant the producer greater prestige); but their fame is also associated with the group to which the pixador belongs, in a form of *vicarious or collective celebrity*. The pixadores refers to this celebrity as *ibope*, a slang word derived from the acronym for *Instituto Brasileiro de Opinão Pública e Estadística*[17] (Araya López, 2015, p. 120). The more *ibope* a pixador gets for the quantity and quality of his/her work, the more prestige and symbolic power he/she enjoys, and the more prestige for his/her group. This status economy needs to be considered to understand the unauthorized and transgressive nature of this controversial practice.

Conclusion

This chapter examines contested and opposed forms of celebrity linked to the world of both street art graffiti and pixação. Brazilian graffiti artists not only enjoy symbolic power but, are sometimes economically rewarded for their work, both on the street and in the formal art market[18]. The emergence of *supergrafiteiros* like OsGemeos with the status of international celebrities does not signify that all graffiti artists in Brazil are en route to this 'self-made' success. The trends of the art market, the advertising industry, and the tastes of the middle and upper classes also have an impact on the celebrity (and the opportunities) that Brazilian street artists can attain. The articles examined demonstrate that street art graffiti is accepted because its aesthetics are easier to digest or because it can be produced in synchrony with the capitalist system (advertising, interior design, book publishing, etc.). These specific graffiti

---

[17] Brazilian Institute of Public Opinion and Statistics, established 1942.

[18] However, several graffiti artworks and murals were removed from the Avenida 23 de Maio as part of an anti-pixação campaign promoted by Mayor João Doria in January 2017. After criticism, Doria promised new spaces for graffiti art and offered to pay for the paint.

productions seem to be preferred and promoted yet, some are still political. Social uses of graffiti as a means of turning (peripheral/urban) youth into entrepreneurs or as a way of fostering self-esteem and a sense of belonging are not unusual in the Brazilian context.

In contrast to this, the practice of pixação is prosecuted and openly opposed, both physically and discursively. Anti-pixação campaigns aim at the eradication of the practice and the use of graffiti as a means to dissuade potential pixadores aims at the eradication of the producers. The transgressive and closed, non-communicative aesthetics and symbols of pixação are partly to blame for the public disdain toward the practice. The pixadores seem to create and produce only for themselves, in a countercultural or subcultural environment, in parallel with the mainstream consumption of other friendlier forms of graffiti or street art. Their interest is not to establish a dialogue with society as a whole, but to 'attack' through transgression. Moreover, the internationalization of pixação and the sudden celebrity enjoyed by a small group of pixadores has created a sort of *superpixadores*, or individuals with a differentiated status, associated with symbolic, economic and political power. While a few pixadores are invited to openings in Paris and Berlin, or are depicted in both national and international films, the majority of the pixadores are part of a practice that is associated with hazardous physical and legal consequences, from imprisonment to death (whether accidental or in encounters with private owners or the police). Unlike graffiti artists, the celebrity of pixadores seems to be linked to a status system that includes not only the individual but, the collective to which the pixador belongs.

This chapter focused exclusively on media content and discourses therefore, no interviews with the pixadores or the graffiti artists are included. Further research is necessary to understand whether the pixadores/graffiti artists consider themselves 'celebrities' or 'activists', as well as to examine their concept of 'social movement'. Considering the transgressive nature of the practice and the forced inclusion of their 'artwork' in both the streets and the artistic institutions, the pixadores seem to be aware of their own power and of the power struggles within these physical and discursive 'spaces'.

Acknowledgments

This chapter is adapted from the doctoral dissertation "*Public spaces, stigmatization and media discourses of graffiti practices in Latin American press: Dynamics of symbolic exclusion and inclusion of urban youth*" (Freie Universität Berlin, 2015), funded by the German Academic Exchange Service (DAAD). I thank the editors and the two anonymous reviewers for their helpful feedback.

References

Altheide, D. (1997) The News Media, the Problem Frame and the Problem of Fear. *The Sociological Quarterly. 38*(4), 647-668.

Araya López (2015). *Public spaces, stigmatization and media discourses of graffiti practices in Latin American press: Dynamics of symbolic exclusion and inclusion of urban youth*. [Online dissertation]. Freie Universität Berlin.

Araujo, T. (2010, March 29). Era uma vez underground. *Folha de São Paulo*. Retrieved from http://www.folha.uol.com.br.

Avritzer, L. & Costa, S. (2004). Teoria crítica, democracia e esfera pública: Concepções e usos na America Latina. *Dados*, *47*(04), Instituto Universitário de Pesquisas do Rio de Janeiro, 703-728.

Austin, J. (2001). *Taking the train. How Graffiti Art became an Urban Crisis in New York City*. New York: Columbia University Press.

Brito, L. (2005, May 18). Plano antipichação tem início com críticas. *Folha de São Paulo*. Retrieved from http://www.folha.uol.com.br.

Capriglione, L. (2008a, June 13). Pichadores vandalizam escola para discutir conceito de arte. *Folha de São Paulo*. Retrieved from http://www.folha.uol.com.br.

Capriglione, L. (2008b, December 20). Ódio a pichadores me deixou tanto tempo presa, afirma jovem. *Folha de São Paulo*. Retrieved from http://www.folha.uol.com.br.

Choque, A. (2008, October 27). Grupo invade prédio da Bienal e picha "andar vazio". *Folha de São Paulo*. Retrieved from http://www.folha.uol.com.br.

de Moraes, A. E. (2003, July 20). A deprimente pichação de São Paulo. *Folha de São Paulo*. Retrieved from http://www.folha.uol.com.br.

Escandari, A. (2014). *Pichadores*. Helsinki-Filmi. [Motion Picture].

Ferrell, J. (1993). *Crimes of Style. Urban Graffiti and the Politics of Criminality*. New York: Garland Publishing, Inc.

Ferrell, J. (1999) Cultural Criminology. *Annual Review of Sociology*. *25*, 395-418.

Francisco, L. (2005, October 30). Salvador transforma pichadores em grafiteiros-servidores. *Folha de São Paulo*. Retrieved from http://www.folha.uol.com.br.

Franco, S. (2009). *Iconografias da Metrópole. Grafiteiros e Pixadores representando o Contemporâneo*. São Paulo: Dissertação Mestrado, Projecto Espaço e Cultura, FAUUSP.

Fraser, N. (1990) Rethinking the Public Sphere: A Contribution to the Critique of Actually Existing Democracy. *Social Text*, *25/26*, 56-80.

Furlaneto, A. (2008, July 4). "Por equívoco", prefeitura apaga painel de artistas. *Folha de São Paulo*. Retrieved from http://www.folha.uol.com.br.

Gonos, G., Mulkern, V., & Poushinsky, N. (1976). Anonymous Expression: A Structural View of Graffiti. *The Journal of American Folklore. 89*(351), 40-48.

Guidry, J. & Sawyer, M. (2003). Contentious Pluralism: The Public Sphere and Democracy. *Perspectives on Politics. 1*(2), 273-289.

Habermas, J. (1990 [1962]) *Strukturwandel der Öffentlichkeit. Untersuchungen zu einer Kategorie der bürgerlichen Gesellschaft.* Frankfurt am Main: Suhrkamp.

Habermas, J. (1996). *Between Facts and Norms Contributions to a Discourse Theory of Law and Democracy.* Trans. W. Rehg. Cambridge: MIT Press.

Harvey, D. (2012). *Rebel Cities. From the Right to the City to the Urban Revolution.* London: Verso.

Kozak, C. (2004). *Contra la pared. Sobre graffitis, pintadas y otras intervenciones urbanas.* Buenos Aires: Libros del Rojas.

Lachmann, R. (1998). Graffiti as Career and Ideology. *American Journal of Sociology. 94*(2), 229-250.

Löw, M. (2001) *Raumsoziologie.* Frankfurt am Main: Suhrkamp.

Löw, M. (2010) *Soziologie der Städte.* Frankfurt am Main: Suhrkamp.

Martins, L. & Naísa, L. (2014, August 5). A Polícia Militar Matou Dois Pixadores no Alto de um Prédio em São Paulo. *Vice.* Retrieved from http://www.vice.com.

Mena, F. (2010, April 15). É permitido pichar. *Folha de São Paulo.* Retrieved from http://www.folha.uol.com.br.

Mercier, D. (2008, September 9). Cerca de 30 pichadores invadem galeria de arte e danificam obras expostas. *Folha de São Paulo.* Retrieved from http://www.folha.uol.com.br.

Muniz, D. (2008, December 5). "Picho para o povo olhar e não gostar", diz jovem presa na Bienal. *Folha de São Paulo.* Retrieved from http://www.folha.uol.com.br.

Nadin, J. & Fioratti, G. (2008, July 27). Prefeitura se retrata por ter apagado grafite em SP. *Folha de São Paulo.* Retrieved from http://www.folha.uol.com.br.

Pinheiro, A. (2001, July 23). Buracos no muro. *Folha de São Paulo.* Retrieved from http://www.folha.uol.com.br.

Stocker, T., Dutcher, L.W., Hargrove, S. M., & Cook, E. A. (1972). Social Analysis of Graffiti. *The Journal of American Folklore. 85*(388), 356-366.

Tonkiss, F. (2004). Analysing text and speech: Content and discourse analysis. In C. Seale (Ed.), *Researching Society and Culture* (pp. 367-382). London: Sage.

Vaz, J. & Martí, S. (2010, September 26). Pichador ataca obra com urubus na Bienal. *Folha de São Paulo.* Retrieved from http://www.folha.uol.com.br.

Ventura, T. (2009). Hip-Hop e grafite: Uma abordagem comparativa entre o Rio de Janeiro e São Paulo. *Análise Social, 44*(192), 605-634.

Wainer, J. (2005, October 30). Os Gêmeos colorem o Cambuci e o mundo. *Folha de São Paulo*. Retrieved from http://www.folha.uol.com.br.

Wainer, J. (2007, June 24). Grafiteiros acusam prefeitura de implantar política antigrafite. *Folha de São Paulo*. Retrieved from http://www.folha.uol.com.br.

Wainer, J. & Oliveira, R. (2009) *Pixo.* [Motion Picture].

Wainer, J. (2012, June 13). Paulista 'picha' curador da Bienal de Berlim. *Folha de São Paulo*. Retrieved from http://www.folha.uol.com.br.

Wilson, J.Q. & Kelling, G.L. (1982, March). Broken Windows. *The Atlantic Magazine*. Retrieved from https://www.theatlantic.com/magazine/archive/1982/03/broken-windows/304465/

Clint Eastwood's Identity Politics

Ronald Strickland

Abstract. Throughout his film career, Clint Eastwood has often acted in and directed films about white males who feel out of place and disrespected in a changing American society characterized by rapid demographic diversification. Voters who sympathize with this sentiment are a key constituency for the Republicans. So, it makes sense that the Mitt Romney campaign would trust Eastwood in the role of featured celebrity endorser at the 2012 Republican Convention. However, Eastwood's performance was so narrowly framed within the assumptions of aggrieved white masculinity, and so unrecognizable in its vulgar parody of President Barack Obama, that it provoked ridicule among the audience of viewers on television and social media. This failed performance, along with Obama's re-election, seemed to confirm that the Republican Party's 'Southern Strategy' of coded appeals to racial prejudice was no longer effective. Then Donald Trump won the 2016 election with a campaign in which insensitivity toward minorities, immigrants and women was a prominent feature. This chapter contextualizes Eastwood's appearance in relation to the politics of white male anxiety about belonging in a multicultural society and the expressions of that anxiety in his films, particularly his early film *The Outlaw Josey Wales*. Eastwood's somewhat nuanced embrace of this articulation of aggrieved white masculinity is compared to Donald Trump's more explicit appeal to the same sentiments.

Keywords: Clint Eastwood, Donald Trump, White Masculinity, Southern Strategy, *The Outlaw Josey Wales*

Introduction

In a memorable moment from the 2012 Republican National Convention, the film actor and director Clint Eastwood made a surprise appearance to endorse candidate Mitt Romney. At the time, Eastwood's speech was widely criticized as incoherent at best and implicitly racist at worst. Now, four years later, Eastwood's racially insensitive awkwardness seems tame by comparison with Donald Trump's insulting statements about minorities, immigrants and women. But Trump and Eastwood share much in common, politically. Both are populists—the heroes of Eastwood's movies are working-class icons, and Trump's anti-globalization message of closed borders and economic protectionism departed from the traditional business-friendly opposition to organized labor and free-trade stance of the Republican Party. However, in American politics, conservative populism always appeals to a racially exclusive populace. In his willingness to violate standards of public discourse in discussing women and minorities Trump, like Eastwood, deployed the Party's 'Southern Strategy', a systematic appeal to disaffected white voters in response to the changing landscape of US politics after the Civil Rights legislation of the 1960s. The simplicity of Trump's appeal to aggrieved white masculinity stands in stark contrast to Eastwood's more nuanced articulation of that theme, but it will be useful to analyze Eastwood's version in order to understand why Trump's crude rhetoric of bigotry was so successful.

The Southern Strategy

After the Civil Rights Act of 1964, which outlawed discrimination based on race, color, religion, sex or national origin, and the Voting Rights Act of 1965, which outlawed practices that prevented African Americans from voting in many southern states, the Republican Party adopted a 'Southern Strategy' to reach out to disaffected white voters. In 1968, Richard Nixon won a close presidential race partly on the strength of his campaign promise to uphold 'law and order' and his opposition to 'forced busing'. Nixon's 'law and order' message mined a vein of rhetoric developed in the Southern resistance to the civil rights movement. At the same time, his opposition to 'forced busing' (of school children to achieve racial balance in previously segregated public schools) resonated among white voters in the North who were uncomfortable sending their children to schools with black students. Busing offered a Northern analog to Southern euphemisms such as 'states' rights' and 'law and order' as a way to express racial prejudice more or less covertly. "The language may have referred to transportation," as Ian Haney Lopez points out, "but the emotional wallop came from defiance toward integration" (2015, p. 23). These covert signals pandering to white resentment function like a dog whistle, "inaudible and easily denied in one range, yet stimulating strong reactions in another" (p. 23). On the one hand, Lopez observes, every politician is ostensibly opposed to racism and eager to condemn those who use the "n-word." Meanwhile, the Republican Party "keeps up a steady drumbeat of subliminal racial grievances and appeals to color-coded solidarity" (p. 4-5).

Lopez notes that Ronald Reagan picked up the rhetoric of the Southern Strategy where Nixon left off. While campaigning for president, he was fond of telling stories featuring readily identifiable anti-black stereotypes about "Cadillac-driving welfare queens" and "strapping young bucks" who bought T-bone steaks with food stamps (p. 4). These coded messages could also be subtler and symbolic, as for example, when Reagan chose a county fair near the small town of Philadelphia, Mississippi as the site from which to announce his 1980 campaign for president. Presidential candidates typically announce their campaigns from locations with some personal or political symbolism, such as their hometown, or a location with special relevance to their political base of support. Reagan had no previous connection to this small southern town, and except for vowing to protect states' rights, he made no mention of a specific political agenda connected with the town. So, one might ask, why the choice of this unlikely spot to launch his campaign? In July of 1964, three young civil rights workers who had been registering African-Americans to vote in the area were arrested and then murdered by local police officers in Philadelphia, Mississippi. The national shame of this small town symbolized the shame of the entire South. Without saying anything explicitly, the Reagan campaign was sending a signal to disaffected white southern voters: "We understand and sympathize with your plight."

By contrast, Trump's appeal to racial prejudice during the 2016 campaign was open and explicit rather than coded and subtle, and it was welcomed as a sign of mainstream acceptance by white supremacists like former Ku Klux Klan leader David Duke and others. At a conference held in Washington, D.C. the week after the election Trump's victory was celebrated with Nazi salutes and cries of "Hail Trump, hail our people, hail victory" by members of the "alt-right" movement promoted by Richard Spencer's National Policy Institute, a white nationalist organization "dedicated to the heritage, identity, and future of people of European descent in the United States, and around the world" (Lombroso & Appelbaum, 2016). Reporting on the event in the *New York Times*, Allen Rappeport and Noah Wieland wrote:

> Hundreds of [Spencer's] extremist supporters . . . gathered for what they had supposed would be an autopsy to plot their grim future under a Clinton administration. Instead, they celebrated the unexpected march of their white nationalist ideas toward the mainstream, portraying Mr. Trump's win as validation that the tide had turned in their fight to preserve white culture. (2016)

The affinity between Trump and the alt-right white nationalist movement was confirmed by one of his first acts as president-elect, naming Stephen Bannon in a key role as "chief strategist and senior counselor" in his White House staff. Bannon is the former president of the conservative media outlet *Breitbart News*. Under his leadership, *Breitbart News* deliberately sought the white nationalist fringe as an audience, becoming the premier media platform of the alt-right movement according to Bannon himself in an interview with *Mother Jones* reporter Sarah Posner (2016). In the following sections, this chapter will identify a thread of white supremacist ideology that runs through Clint Eastwood's film career, and will suggest that Trump's ethno-nationalist turn is not a departure but an intensification of a theme that was on display in Eastwood's performance at the 2012 Republican Convention. Trump's connection to the white supremacist movement is not a coincidence, but part of a conscious strategy. Trump appeals to many voters, not despite his willingness to say politically incorrect things about minorities, immigrants and women, but precisely because he says things that would have been seen as disqualifying gaffes in previous years.

Eastwood's Invisible Obama

It would have been difficult to predict at the time, coming after the election of the nation's first black president, but Eastwood's 2012 Convention speech can now be seen as a harbinger of Trump's successful campaign. Eastwood spoke as a "surprise celebrity endorser," shortly before candidate Mitt Romney himself accepted the nomination. In the sequence, which can be viewed on YouTube (ABC News, 2012), Eastwood held a pretended conversation with an empty chair that was meant to represent an absent President Barack Obama. Eastwood begins by asking the "invisible Obama" how he handles questions about broken campaign promises, such as why he has not yet closed "Gitmo," the internment camp at Guantanamo Bay. Then, without relaying a purported answer, he pretends to have been told to shut up: "What's that? I'm not going to shut up. It's my turn." A moment later, after mentioning that Mitt Romney had proposed that the troops should be brought home from Afghanistan "tomorrow morning", Eastwood pretends that Obama has made a vulgar response to him: "What? What do you want me to tell Romney? I can't tell him to do that. He can't do that to himself" (ABC News, 2012).

Why, many observers asked, did the Republicans turn the prime-time stage over to such a stumbling, unpredictable speaker? Why did they allow him to speak extemporaneously, in sharp contrast to the tightly controlled scripting of other speakers? In the aftermath, Eastwood remarked that "if somebody's dumb enough to ask me to say something, they're gonna have to take what they get." "What the Republicans got," Halperin and Heilemann write, "was an object lesson in the dangers of celebrity casting" (2013, p. 375). However, they also got a dog whistle appeal to racial resentment that backfired in 2012, because it was too easily identifiable as a racially prejudiced and unfairly insulting attack against President Obama. Eastwood's convention appearance invoked a vague articulation of white supremacist identity politics and white working-class anger at financial and political elites, neither of which Mitt Romney could comfortably embrace. In 2016, Donald Trump broadened the range of racist (and sexist) sentiments in American political campaigns to an extent that made Eastwood's performance seem tame by comparison.

74   R. Strickland

The Outlaw Josey Wales

If the politics of white male vulnerability and anger at elites were awkwardly expressed by Eastwood the celebrity, they are skillfully elaborated in many of his films, including and especially in his early film *The Outlaw Josey Wales*, released in 1976. Eastwood portrays a former confederate guerilla fighter who makes common cause with Native Americans in opposition to the federal government. The film's diagetic frame invokes a pleasant myth of amity between Europeans and Native Americans, implicitly suggesting that this entitles certain whites (defeated Confederates and disaffected Southerners, in this case) to lay claim to a comparable experience of suffering and oppression. The effect is to counter or diminish the victim status of historically oppressed minorities such as African Americans and also, ironically, of Native Americans, too.

The film is set in the late 1860s, just after the Civil War. In the opening scenes we learn that the protagonist, Josey Wales, has been a farmer in the Missouri Ozarks before the war. One day his house was burned and his wife and child were killed by a band of "Jayhawkers"—anti-slavery marauders from Kansas. Seeking revenge, Josey Wales has joined a Missouri group of pro-Confederate raiders. At the end of the war, he has refused to surrender, and he has been declared a wanted outlaw. In order to escape capture Wales leaves Missouri, crossing into the Indian territory of Oklahoma. There he meets and teams up with Lone Watie, a Cherokee man who, like Wales, has been dispossessed of his home and has lost his family. Together, they make their way toward Texas, picking up some fellow refugees—both white and indigenous—along the way. In Texas, settling on an isolated ranch, they are confronted by a band of Comanche Indians whose traditional lands they are usurping. With his small community vastly outnumbered, Josey Wales rides out alone to meet Ten Bears, the leader of the Comanche band. Having heard of Josey Wales' reputation as a courageous fighter against the United States government, Ten Bears feels an instinctive affinity with him and agrees to a truce. They seal the pact by becoming "blood brothers."

This scene was clearly on Eastwood's mind as he came to the convention. According to Halperin and Heilemann, he brought with him a DVD video clip depicting this encounter between Josey Wales and Ten Bears, with Ten Bears saying "It's sad that governments are chiefed by the double-tongues." Eastwood suggested that the clip be used in his introduction. In the event, it was not used, but his image as 'Josey Wales' was projected on the screen behind him as he began to speak. Meanwhile, the convention crowd repeatedly shouted out to urge him to deliver his famous line from the *Dirty Harry* movies: 'Go ahead…make my day.' In choosing the less familiar image of Josey Wales rather than Harry Callahan, Eastwood may have sought to articulate a libertarian or anti-federal government stance along the lines of Ten Bears' statement, combined with a suggestion of multicultural solidarity. By contrast, the crowd's request for the 'make my day' line recalls Reagan's use of the phrase and also a more straightforward affirmation of violent authoritarianism. In any case, Eastwood's reluctance to utter the phrase says something of the difficulty of articulating those politics as a politically-engaged celebrity, rather than in a film. This will be discussed further, later in the chapter.

Cherokee Racial Politics

Along with the representation of Indians as wild, dangerous and sometimes noble savages, narratives of friendship, trust and respect between European-Americans and Native Americans have long been a staple of mainstream popular culture. Such fanciful narratives are rightly subordinated to the overall pattern of oppression by historians—as the Native American writer Vine DeLoria once observed, if every white person who claimed to have an Indian princess as an ancestor were telling the truth, "most tribes would have been entirely female for the first three hundred years of white occupation" (1988, p. 3). However, this picture comes perhaps nearest the truth in the historical record of the so-called 'Five Civilized Tribes'—the Cherokee, Chickasaw, Choctaw, Creek, and Seminole—who originally occupied the southeastern United States. These tribes were considered "civilized" by white Americans because they embraced European customs and religion. Many Cherokees, whose traditional lands were in the region of the former Confederacy, adopted Euro-American lifestyles, the English language and Christianity. Cherokees entered mainstream trade and business ventures, sometimes becoming wealthy plantation owners in the ante-bellum South. However, by the 1820s, there was increasing tension between whites and Cherokees prompted by white immigration into Georgia.

In 1830, President Andrew Jackson signed into law the Indian Removal Act, and began a process of forced relocation of the Cherokees from their traditional lands in Georgia and other southeastern states to the western territory of Oklahoma. Between 1831 and 1838, more than 45,000 Native Americans were relocated by forced march. This event, which became known as the 'Trail of Tears,' included 15,000 Cherokees (Jahoda, 1995). More than 4,000 of them died on the journey. So, it is easy to understand Cherokee bitterness toward the federal government. Associating Cherokees – historically and in the present – with white racism is seemingly complicated. In fact, most of the Cherokee tribal leadership supported the Confederacy during the Civil War, Brigadier General Stand Watie, a Cherokee, whose fictional namesake, Lone Watie, appears as the Cherokee character in *The Outlaw Josey Wales*. Historian Arrell Morgan Gibson has given a detailed account of the political and economic bases for the alliance. Most immediately, during the 1860 presidential campaign Republican politician William Seward, who would later become President Lincoln's Secretary of State, attempted to appeal to 'free-soil' voters by advocating a policy to take the Oklahoma territory from the Five Civilized Tribes and make it available to white settlers. Further, in the spring of 1861, anticipating trouble with secessionists, Seward ordered the abandonment of all posts in Indian Territory (Oklahoma). This violated existing treaty pledges, and left the Cherokees and other relocated tribes vulnerable to attack from the Confederacy. Further, The Republicans in power were opposed to slavery; many wealthy and influential Cherokees and other tribal leaders were slave-holders and stood to lose substantial wealth if slavery were to be abolished (Gibson, 1958, p. 387-8).

This articulation of antipathy toward the federal government and complicity with anti-black racism remains current in contemporary Cherokee tribal politics. In the 2010 US census, there were 300,000 Americans registered as members of the three Cherokee groups recognized by the federal government (Crow, 2012). This number includes more than 2,000 disputed members— black Cherokees or 'Freedmen'—who are descendants of African Americans held in slavery by wealthy Cherokees before the Civil War. After the Civil War the Cherokee Nation signed a treaty with the federal government according to which their slaves were freed and given full citizenship rights as tribal members. Yet, this settlement remains a matter of controversy to the present day. In recent legal actions, some Cherokee factions have sought to exclude the Freedmen, arguing that (along the lines of the 'states-rights' position of the Confederacy and Southern segregationists) as a sovereign nation, the tribe has the right to self-determination of its citizenship requirements. As Circe Sturm explains, this obsession with race results partly from the broader public's association of "Indian-ness" with race—there is a concern among some Cherokees "that the appearance of racial dilution may threaten their political recognition and eventually their sovereignty" (Sturm, 2014, p. 583). However, the anxiety about Cherokee racial purity is expressed as anti-black prejudice; there is no comparable concern about racial dilution through Cherokee-European mixtures (Mays, 2015).

Asa Carter and the Ku Klux Klan

This digression into Cherokee racial politics is included in order to establish the context for introducing Eastwood's artistic and political association with Asa Carter, one of the cleverest political propagandists of the twentieth century.

Carter was a Ku Klux Klan leader who came to prominence in opposition to the civil rights movement. During the late 1950s he disseminated anti-Semitic and anti-black propaganda through a syndicated radio program in Alabama. In the early 1960s he was a speech-writer for segregationist politician George Wallace; he is credited with having written a famous line from Wallace's 1963 inaugural speech: "segregation now, segregation tomorrow, segregation forever…" (Wallace, 1963). However, Carter seems to have been such a strident racist that even the politician with a platform of racial segregation did not want to be associated with him in public. When Wallace ran for president in 1968 he sought to reach out to a more mainstream national audience, and Carter was not part of the campaign team.

Carter later re-invented himself. He moved to Texas, adopted the name 'Bedford Forrest Carter', and began to tell people that he was a Cherokee. In 1973, he self-published a novel called *The Rebel Outlaw Josey Wales*. Carter sent his novel, unsolicited, to Clint Eastwood, who liked it and adapted the story for the film *The Outlaw Josey Wales*. Notably, the word 'rebel' was deleted from the title of the film version of the novel. There is no evidence that Eastwood knew about Carter's Ku Klux Klan activities. Yet, the Josey Wales character represents a theme of heroic but misunderstood white masculinity that was to become a staple of Eastwood's films.

Noting Carter's "peculiar elision of Confederate outlaw and Indian," Shari Huhnsdorf quotes the following passage from Carter's *Gone to Texas*:

> The mountain man did not have the "land hunger" of the flatlander who had instigated the government's action [the forced relocation of the Cherokees from their lands in the late 1830s]. He preferred the mountains to remain wild…free, unfettered by law and the irritating hypocrisy of organized society. His kinship, therefore, was closer to the Cherokee than to his racial brothers of the flatlands who strained mightily at placing the yoke of society upon their necks… [The Cherokee's] code was the loyalty of the mountain man with all his clannishness…When the War Between the States had burst over the nation, the Cherokee naturally sided with the Confederacy against the hated government that had deprived him of his mountain home. (2011, p. 142-3)

As Huhnsdorf goes on to point out, these 'affinities' are highly contrived— Southern whites had eagerly supported and participated in the Cherokee removal from Georgia, for example. Carter over-states a distinction between 'mountain men' and 'flatlanders' in order to preserve a portion of 'good' Southerners, and by singling out 'clannishness' as a trait shared by both southern mountain men and Cherokees he slyly inserts an allusion to the Ku Klux Klan.

Carter was attempting to articulate a resistance narrative to counter the emerging hegemonic ideology of equal rights, affirmative action and anti-racism. If ranged on a continuum the articulation might be represented as follows:

White Men-Heroes-Rebels-Native Americans-Misunderstood Victims

Eastwood adopts this articulation in his film, and the Romney campaign was not mistaken if they invited Eastwood to speak on the assumption that Eastwood's association with characters representing aggrieved white masculinity would appeal to many voters. However, relatively few voters in 2012 would have consciously recognized the connection to Native Americans in the use of the Josey Wales image by itself. So, Eastwood's over-reliance on the imagery and the campaign's decision not to use the Ten Bears clip contributed to the failure of the performance. Just as Asa Carter was a more successful propagandist as a novelist than he was as a Ku Klux Klan leader, radio broadcaster, or political speech-writer. Eastwood is a better propagandist as a film-maker than he is as a celebrity political endorser.

Reverse Racism and White Redemption

Eastwood's attachment to the concept of aggrieved white masculinity is evident, paradoxically, even in *Bird*, his 1988 film about the career of black jazz saxophonist Charlie Parker. In Eastwood's treatment, the Charlie Parker story becomes a familiar Hollywood narrative of tragically misunderstood artistic genius, ignoring the factor of systemic racism as a possible contributing factor leading to Parker's substance abuse and early death. Moreover, the film presents an inverted representation of the segregated South in which Parker has to pass off Red Rodney, his white trumpet player, as an albino black in order for him to be allowed to perform "in clubs where blacks take the dance floor and whites are confined to cramped balconies away from the action" (1988). This is a strangely counter-historical representation, as Paul Smith observes:

> The site of segregation is the black community, which we are to assume, will not accept a white man into it…[it] is a kind of rhetorical formation that might be familiar to us today, where, in a sick parody of the term *racism*, African-Americans are increasingly often accused of *reverse racism*. (1993, p. 233)

In line with a similar counter-hegemonic logic, the hero of the five *Dirty Harry* films is not simply a racist. Instead, Eastwood gives us an 'underdog' white protagonist whose relationship to the dominant social order is in some sense articulated as being in solidarity with women or minorities. For example, in *Dirty Harry*, the first film in that series, Detective Harry Callahan is assigned to stop a serial killer named Scorpio who is targeting victims that are identifiably 'liberal' or 'weak' stereotypes of people who need to be protected by a violence-prone strong white man—a young woman, a gay black man, a Catholic priest, and a school bus full of children. In other films like *Million-Dollar Baby* (2004) and *Gran Torino* (2008) Eastwood has given us embittered and openly sexist or racist white male protagonists who are redeemed, finally, as they rise above their prejudices to act nobly in support of a woman or an Asian immigrant (who is still, nonetheless, subordinated to the white male hero). When one of Eastwood's film characters says something racist or sexist, there is a dramatic trajectory leading toward redemption. When Eastwood the celebrity expresses those same attitudes, we are stuck with an uncomfortable static reality. The nuanced representation of aggrieved white masculinity in Eastwood's films is more readily accepted than the raw public expression of that sentiment by a celebrity. Or at least that seemed to be the case until Trump proved otherwise in 2016.

Trump and the Southern Strategy

Donald Trump has a long history of public statements that invoke racist sentiments. In 1989, after five black and Latino teenagers who became known as the 'Central Park Five' were arrested and charged with having raped a white woman in New York's Central Park, Trump spent US$85,000 paying for full-page newspaper advertisements calling for the return of the death penalty in New York. "Though he didn't refer to the teenagers by name," Sarah Burns wrote in a *Times* opinion piece in October of 2016, "it was clear to anyone in the city that he was referring to them" (2016). The teenagers were convicted and sent to prison, but in 2003, their convictions were overturned after a confession by another man who said that he had committed the rape alone. DNA evidence substantiated this confession, but no DNA linked the teenagers to the crime. In 2014, New York City settled a US$41 million wrongful conviction suit with the Central Park Five, but Trump still refused to accept the possibility that they were innocent (Holmes, 2016).

"It's not clear why Trump would decide to delve back into this painful episode," wrote *Huffington Post* reporter Matt Ferner, "especially considering he played a distinct role in contributing to the case's racial undertones and apparent clamor for mob justice at the time" (2016). In the same vein, New York Times reporter Michael Barbaro struggled to understand why Trump questioned President Obama's birth-place (and hence, his legitimacy as president) for several years after Obama had released his birth certificate proving that he was born in Hawaii, not in Kenya. "Much has been made of Mr. Trump's casual elasticity with the truth," Barbaro wrote, "…But this lie was different from the start, an insidious, calculated calumny that sought to undo the embrace of an African-American president by the 69 million voters who elected him in 2008" (Barbaro, 2016). Perplexed by Trump's unabashed disingenuousness, Barbaro concludes:

> The essential question – Why promote a lie? – may be unanswerable. Was it sport? Was it his lifelong quest to court media attention? Was it racism? Was it the cynical start of his eventual campaign for president? (2016)

This conclusion—that a successful presidential candidate would base his campaign largely on an open appeal to racial prejudice—is so alien to Ferner, Barbaro, and most of their readers that they are reluctant to make the assertion. Meanwhile, on the campaign trail, Hillary Clinton offered her answer. Rather than being embarrassed by his racial prejudices, Trump was determined to emphasize them: "He has spent this entire campaign offering a dog whistle to his most hateful supporters. He re-tweets white supremacists and spreads racially tinged conspiracy theories. And you better believe he is being heard loudly and clearly" (Lee & Merica, 2016). The only part that Clinton got wrong was in labeling Trump's message a dog whistle; Trump shows little concern to hide his racial prejudice. Over the past several decades the Republicans have managed to thrive in an era of identity politics with coded appeals to a sense of aggrieved white masculinity. Identity politics assumes that oppressed and victimized groups have rights based on past exploitation. There is a moral logic to this assumption. Where it begins to run afoul of both morality and logic is when it is appropriated by those who do not have a legitimate historical claim. It should be recognized that there is always a connection to white supremacist ideology in this articulation, whether it is submerged, as in Eastwood's films and his connection to Ku Klux Klan leader Asa Carter, or flaunted, like Trump's deliberately provocative pronouncements and his close association with alt-right fellow-traveler Stephen Banner.

References

ABC News (2012, August 30). Clint Eastwood RNC speech (complete): Actor assails Obama through empty chair. Retrieved from https://www.youtube.com/watch?v=933hKyKNPFQ.

Barbaro, M. (2016, September 16). Donald Trump clung to 'birther' lie for years, and still isn't apologetic. *New York Times*. Retrieved from https://www.nytimes.com/2016/09/17/us/politics/donald-trump-obama-birther.html?_r=0

Burns, S. (2016, October 16). Why Trump doubled down on the Central Park Five. *New York Times*. Retrieved from: https://www.nytimes.com/2016/10/18/opinion/why-trump-doubled-down-on-the-central-park-five.html?_r=0

Carter, A. (2008). *Gone to Texas* (Originally self-published in 1973 as *The rebel outlaw Josey Wales*). Mattetuck, New York: Amereon Limited.

Crow, Todd (2012, February 21). Census shows increase in Cherokee respondents. *Cherokee Phoenix.* Retrieved from http://www.cherokeephoenix.org/ Article/Index/ 5990.

Deloria, V. (1988). *Custer died for your sins: An Indian manifesto.* Norman: U of Oklahoma Press.

Eastwood, C. (Director). (1976). *The outlaw Josey Wales* [Motion Picture]. United States: Malpaso Productions.

Eastwood, C. (Director). (1988). *Bird* [Motion Picture]. United States: Warner Brothers Pictures.

Eastwood, C. (Director). (2004). *Million-dollar baby* [Motion Picture]. United States: Warner Brothers Pictures.

Eastwood, C. (Director). (2008) *Gran Torino* [Motion Picture]. United States: Warner Brothers Pictures.

Ferner, M. (2016, October 7). Donald Trump still thinks the Central Park Five are guilty (they aren't). *Huffington Post*. Retrieved from http://www.huffingtonpost. com/entry/donald-trump-central-park-five_us_57f7ceafe4b0e655eab3c002.

Gibson, A. M. (1985). Native Americans and the Civil War. *American Indian Quarterly*, *9*(4), 385-410.

Halperin, M. & Heilemann, J. (2013). *Double down: Game change 2012*. New York: Penguin.

Heilemann, J. (2015, November 2). With All Due Respect: Interview with Donald Trump. *Bloomberg News*. Retrieved from https://www.youtube.com/watch?v=TYP 8I7ERUas.

Holmes, S. A. (2016, October 7). Member of 'Central Park 5' blasts Trump. *CNN Politics*. Retrieved from http://www.cnn.com/2016/10/06/politics/reality-check-donald-trump-central-park-5/.

Huhndorf, S. (2001). *Going Native: Indians in the American Cultural Imagination.* Ithaca: Cornell University Press.

Jahoda, G. (1995). *The Trail of tears.* New York: Wings Press.

Kessler, G. (2016, March 1). Donald Trump and David Duke: For the record. *Washington Post.* Retrieved from https:washingtonpost.com/news/fact-checker/wp/ 2016/03/01/donald-trump-and-david-duke-for-the-record/.

Kneeland, D. (1980, August 4). Reagan campaigns at Mississippi fair: Nominee tells crowd of 10,000 he is backing states' rights. *New York Times*. Retrieved from http://

query.nytimes.com/mem/archivefree/pdf?res=9800E2D7103BE732A25757A9E9C 9D 6CF.

Lee, M. J. & Merica, D. (2016, November 3). Central Park Five and the KKK: Clinton paints Trump as a racist. *CNN Politics*. Retrieved from http://www.cnn. com/2016/11/03/politics/hillary-clinton-donald-trump-african-americans/.

Lombroso, D. & Appelbaum, Y. (2016, November 21). 'Hail Trump!': White nationalists salute the president elect. *The Atlantic*. Retrieved from http://www.the atlantic.com/politics/archive/2016/11/richard-spencer-speech-npi/508379/.

Mays, K. (2015, July 20). Still waiting: Cherokee freedmen say they're not going anywhere. *Indian Country News.* Retrieved from http://indiancountrytodaymedianet work.com/2015/07/20/still-waiting-cherokee-freedman-say-theyre-not-going anywhere-161132.

Native News Online Staff. (2014, May 5). Cherokee freedmen lawsuit update: Cherokee nation presents oral arguments in US District Court in Washington. Retrieved from http://nativenewsonline.net/currents/cherokee-freedmen-lawsuit-up date-cherokee-nation-presents-oral-arguments-us-district-court-washington/.

Posner, S. (2016, August 22). How Donald Trump's new campaign chief created an online haven for white nationalists. *Mother Jones*. Retrieved from http://www. motherjones.com/politics/2016/08/stephen-bannon-donald-trump-alt-right-breitbart-news.

Rappeport, A, & Wieland, N. (2016, November 19). White nationalists celebrate "an awakening" after Trump's victory. *New York Times*. Retrieved from http:// www. nytimes.com/2016/11/20/us/politics/white-nationalists-celebrate-an-awakening-after-donald-trumps-victory.html.

Smith, P. (1993). *Clint Eastwood: A cultural production*. Minneapolis: University of Minnesota Press.

Sturm, C. (2014). Race, sovereignty, and civil rights: Understanding the Cherokee freedmen controversy. *Cultural Anthropology, 29*(3), 575-98.

Wallace, G. (1963). Inaugural address of Governor George Wallace, which was delivered at the Capitol in Montgomery, Alabama. *Alabama Textual Materials Collection*. Retrieved from http://digital.archives.alabama.gov/ cdm/singleitem/collection/voices/id/2952/rec/5

Rebel with a Cause: Celebrity, Authenticity and Political Capital

Tomasz Olczyk and Jacek Wasilewski

Abstract: In the world of millennials, one of the fundamental qualities is authenticity. Political sphere is no exception. Thanks to his authenticity, a rebel rock man with no real political programme, no prior political party allegiance and lacking substantial funds for running his political campaign has won 20% of votes in the Polish presidential election. He has set up his own political organization, which in turn has gained 9% backing in the parliamentary election. How did a celebrity with no political platform, no media backing, and no party structure achieved such a notable result in the presidential election, created political movement and led his movement candidates to the parliament? This chapter explains this phenomenon with recourse to the analysis of Facebook communication and the reconstruction of his message and political image archetype.

Keywords: Celebritization, celebrity-candidate, political capital, authenticity

Introduction

The Paweł Kukiz case is interesting not only because of his record-breaking electoral result but most importantly for two qualitative novelties it brings to celebrity politics studies. First of all, unlike other celebrity politicians, Kukiz created his own successful political organization – 'Kukiz' 15 Movement' – around his personal brand. Hence, he broadened the standard taxonomy of political celebrities by adding a new category: 'celebrity political organizer'. Secondly, some elements of the celebrity image are often a liability for celebrities who seek legislative or executive offices and want to be seen as serious politicians. Kukiz' celebrity image was his key advantage and the main source of his political capital. Furthermore, the more his image was politicized, the more popular support he lost (see fig.1).

The brief political career of Kukiz resembles a rollercoaster. He gained unexpected successes at the president election, failed at the referendum and managed a last minute comeback during parliamentary elections. It is a political trajectory that seems difficult to explain. This chapter argues that the main factor in his success in the presidential election was synergy between his populist political message and his celebrity rebel persona. This synergy allowed Kukiz to be seen as an authentic spokesperson for three million of the youngest voters. His authenticity started to vanish after he had become involved in the 'politics as usual'. Therefore, after the voting system referendum failure he engaged in a sophisticated branding campaign in order to remind his voters of his rock stage roots and to regain authenticity (see fig 2.). This strategy proved to be at least partially effective as 'Kukiz'15 Movement' was saved from the brink of electoral defeat and gained a 9% backing in the parliamentary election. This chapter is divided into six parts. Firstly, it describes Paweł Kukiz' road from punk vocalist to presidential candidate and a Member of Parliament. The second part presents the methodological approach and materials on which the analysis is based. Then, using collective action framing theory (Benford & Snow, 2000) Kukiz' political message is described. The next part is devoted to Kukiz' image, exploiting twelve brand archetypes theory to show how he used his celebrity persona to activate the rebel brand (Pearson & Mark, 2001). This is followed by an analysis of the rhetorical and branding devices he used to regain authenticity previously lost due to his involvement in party politics. In conclusion the chapter discusses the novelties of the Kukiz case and the paradoxes of celebrity political commitment.

From Punk to Presidential Candidate

Paweł Kukiz, vocalist, born in 1963, reached adulthood in the late Communist era in Poland. His initial punk rock projects were alternative to the pop music mainstream controlled by the Communist authorities. After the downfall of Communism his work became diversified and at the same time - popular and folk. Kukiz also featured in a few movies and theatre plays. Among others, he played Che Guevara in the Polish version of *Evita*. After 1989, he remained a popular musician, though he would not exactly be named among the top artists of the Polish pop scene.

The political profile of his work cannot be easily defined as either right-wing or leftist. In 1997, he provoked a scandal by an anticlerical song directed against the right-wing. Seven years later he became famous for his song, which hit the leftist post-Communist party. The greatest Kukiz hit was, however, the love song 'Skóra' (Skin), with anti-discriminatory overtones, dating back to the 1980s. It seems that Kukiz' texts have no common denominator in terms of the author's coherent ideological background but are rooted in his opposition to the current political and cultural mainstream (Stankiewicz, 2015, p. 1-30).

Kukiz' way to politics was initially a typical pathway for a celebrity (Street, 2004, p. 437-438; Marsh, 't Hart & Tindall, 2010, p. 327). Since 1997, he started to publicly endorse various – though mainly right-wing – political parties and candidates. Around 2011, he became involved in a grassroots movement promoting changes to the voting system; to majority voting with a single-member district. In 2014, he won a seat in the regional council transforming from a celebrity-advocate into a celebrity–politician. A group of his closest advisers and associates came up with the idea of Kukiz running for President at the following election (Stankiewicz, 2015, p. 1-30). The Presidential election turned into the referendum on Civic Platform (CP) governance. After eight years of CP rule and five years of the Bronisław Komorowski's Presidency, voters started to look for an alternative. For many of them this alternative came in the form of the conservative Law & Justice (L&J) party and its young and energetic Presidential nominee, Andrzej Duda. Nonetheless, many people were disappointed not only with the party at the helm but also with the whole political class. This part of the electorate became the core of Kukiz' target group. In February 2015, Paweł Kukiz officially declared his candidacy. Right from the start he framed his presidential bid as an advocacy campaign for the reform of the voting system to a simple-majority one with single-seat constituency.

The Kukiz staff adopted the tools, communication and organizational strategies typical of grassroots campaigns for candidates from outside of the establishment who lacked the financial and organizational backing of political parties (Trippi, 2009). Online, Kukiz' associates collected the much needed signatures that allowed Kukiz to officially register as a candidate. The candidate himself used Facebook as the main channel to communicate with his supporters. Initial support for Kukiz fluctuated in the polls at around a few percent, very close to the sampling error (see fig.1.). An acute criticism of the political elites and the stage charisma shown during his meetings with the voters started to attract the attention of those discouraged and disenchanted with the structured parties. In March, his backing was 2% and in April it reached 6%. Ultimately, in the first voting he obtained 20.8% of the votes against the 33.8% figure of the incumbent president and 34.8% of Andrzej Duda (Państwowa Komisja Wyborcza, 2015a). Since none of the candidates managed to get an absolute majority, the end of May saw a second round of voting. The then-incumbent President, while seeking the support of three million of Kukiz voters, declared a referendum on the single seat constituency. The main goal of the advocacy campaign of Paweł Kukiz seemed to be achieved.

Kukiz and his inner circle strived to exploit the success of the Presidential election in the referendum to follow and in the parliamentary election (Palade, 2015). In order to co-ordinate the referendum campaign and make an official debut during the parliamentary elections they started creating an organizational structure. In Kukiz's narrative, 'political party' was synonymous with cynicism and the lack of authenticity. Therefore, he emphasized the fact that his new organization is a grassroots social movement. The name and the brand of the movement, 'Kukiz'15 Movement', exploited the recognition and success of Kukiz' presidential elections committee brand: 'Kukiz 15'. By setting up his own political organization, Kukiz broadened the classical typology of celebrity politicians and became a celebrity – the political organizer. The early polls showed an uptrend of 'Kukiz'15 Movement'. It seemed that, spurred on by the referendum campaign and by the CP crisis, Kukiz's initiative stood a good chance of becoming the second force in the parliament. However, in the following months Kukiz' movement started to lose some of its support. The September referendum on a single-seat constituency proved to be an utter disaster for Kukiz' movement. The turnout was the lowest in the history of the 3rd Republic. Although the majority voted in favour of Kukiz' suggested initiative, the number of voters was too small for the vote to be binding in parliament (Państwowa Komisja Wyborcza, 2015b). Meanwhile, the support for the 'Kukiz'15 Movement' began to decline to the 5% electoral threshold. Ultimately, in October 2015 the Kukiz movement made its way into the parliament with 9% of the votes, just a third of the backing declared only in June of that year (Państwowa Komisja Wyborcza, 2015c).

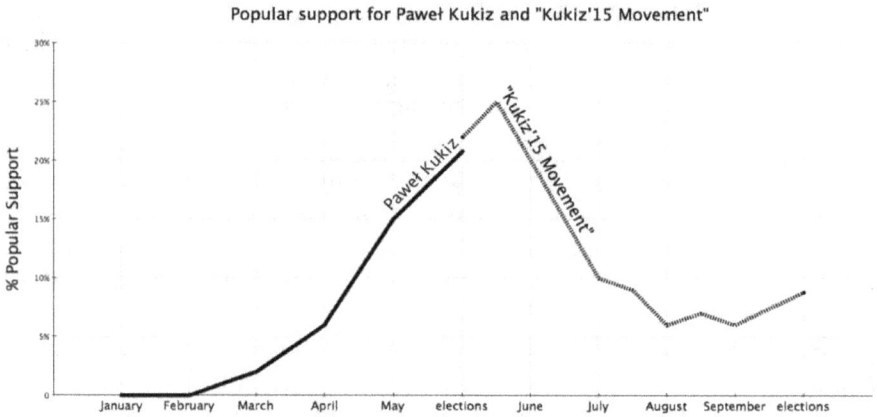

Fig. 1. Popular support for Paweł Kukiz in presidential campaign and for "Kukiz'15 Movement" in parliamentary campaign, sources: for presidential elections (Maliszewski, 2015), for parliamentary election (Palade, 2015)

Methods and Material

In order to understand Kukiz and the phenomenon of his political movement, we applied collective action frames theory. This concept is used in sociology for researching social movements (Benford & Snow, 2000). The frames of collective action are schemes through which social movements construct common definitions of social problems and the ways of resolving them (2000,

p. 615-616). Explaining the present state through this concept is carried out with the use of the so-called diagnostic frame. This involves identification of a problem, its sources, causes, and the culprits (2000, p. 616). The solution to the problem described by the diagnostic frame is called prognostic framing. The analysis of social movements are often accompanied by marked articulation of suggested problem solutions (2000, p. 616).

The main source of Kukiz' message was his Facebook profile. Facebook proved to be a particularly significant channel of communication for Kukiz who used it as a way of circumventing the filters and frames of the mainstream media, which he put under constant criticism. We analyzed the posts published on his official profile between January and October of 2015 (400 posts all together).

Secondly, we have taken a look at how Kukiz' image was constructed. From the voter's viewpoint, the campaign is a process of comparing candidates (Popkin, 1994). Voters construct the image of a candidate seeking out differences and similarities. In order to describe the system of meanings activated by Kukiz during his presidential election campaign, we compared his image with the meanings constructed by his two main rivals: incumbent President Bronisław Komorowski and his L&J opponent Andrzej Duda. Duda and Komorowski served as contrasting figures for voters and helped them to construct a certain image of Kukiz. This choice also has a quantitative justification. The two mentioned and Kukiz have won over altogether 87% of the total votes in the first round of the election.

In our analysis of Kukiz's persona we have applied the Liesbet Van Zoonen typology of political personae (Van Zoonen, 2005, p. 82-85) and the concept of the twelve brand archetypes (Pearson & Mark, 2001). Van Zoonen's typology is based on the two dimensions of celebrity politics, i.e. outsider–insider and ordinary–special (2005, p. 82-85). The key idea in the theory of twelve brand archetypes is an archetype understood as culturally structured bundles of needs. According to Pearson and Mark these needs can be depicted on two axes: affiliation-independence and stability–risk. Various combinations of motivations mean that there can be twelve fundamental archetypes of brands singled out. Archetypes related to the need for stability and control are the archetypes of Creator, Caregiver and Ruler. The need for affiliation is accomplished by: Jester, Every Man and Lover. Risk is reflected in the Hero, Rebel, and Magician; whereas independence is represented by the archetypes of Innocent, Explorer, and Sage (Pearson & Mark, 2001, p. 22).

Televised political advertisements provided material for the analysis of Kukiz' image and the images of his contenders. Concise, audiovisual, fully controlled message of political spots provides an excellent insight into the techniques of the candidates' self-presentation. In this case, we have compared the messages of Kukiz and of his Movement with the messages of his opponents, broadcast on the first and last day of the campaign.

Message – Diagnostic and Prognostic Frames

The diagnostic frame used by Kukiz may be labeled by his own term: "particracy" (Kukiz, 2015f). Particracy served in Kukiz's communication as a short description of all the dysfunctions of Polish politics as well as the cause of social and economic problems. In his opinion, party divisions are fictitious and in reality they serve only to divide the society. According to Kukiz' message, the party elites simulate a staged conflict. That staged ritual serves to turn people's attention away from the real conflict between ordinary people and the party oligarchy. As he wrote in his typical style:

> This whole Polish political 'stage' is an embarrassment... 'Circus' would be much better term to describe them... Nothing is going on there. Just smoke and mirrors, show, creation... They 'elect' themselves from among themselves... Surely there is a fight there... But only internal... For positions. (Kukiz, 2015c)

The nation is exploited not only by the local political forces but also by the global economic powers. As he wrote on his Facebook wall: "For 26 years Poland has been drained by multinational corporations...We have to reclaim our country for the Citizens!" (Kukiz, 2015e).

According to Kukiz, the party elites manipulate people's emotions by creating artificial divisions. In reality they cooperate and realize their own party interests, often contrary to the interests of the society, nation and the state. In Kukiz' message, the uncontrolled rule of the political oligarchy is enabled by the voting system. The Polish election system is characterized by proportional representation in which the parties, or rather – according to Kukiz – their strict elites holding power, decide which names to put on the candidate lists. According to Kukiz, this substantially limits the passive voting right of ordinary people not belonging to the political oligarchy. In consequence, it makes free election a fiction.

The solution – prognostic frame – of Kukiz movement was the majority system with single seat constituency. In this way the citizens would be able to opt for the specific persons and not the party list. Passive voting right shall not be limited by party oligarchs drawing up the election lists. Hence, the reform of the voting system would take the power away from the party oligarchs and bring it back into the hands of the citizens (Kukiz, 2015d).

Messenger – Celebrity Persona and Authenticity

The diagnostic frame, as promoted by Kukiz in his political communication, was nothing novel. Certain elements framing the political system of the 3rd Polish Republic as a conspiracy of the party elites as manifested by Kukiz had been present in the messages of numerous candidates running for Oresidency and in many populist political party platforms since the downfall of Communism (Olczyk, 2009; Wasilewski, 2012). However, none of those candidates or parties claimed a three million vote success in the election. In our opinion, the celebrity persona of the messenger was a key factor. Hence, the second aspect which we analyse in our text is that of the messenger. In our work we focused predominantly on the persona of Paweł Kukiz, the aspects, which made him stand apart from the less effective messengers of the similar diagnostic frame and also on the major characteristic features of his image in the presidential campaign.

First of all, in line with Van Zoonen's typology of political personae, it can be said that unlike his anti-establishement populist predecessors, Kukiz was an authentic outsider; a person completely new to politics. His political career boiled down to just somewhat over a year at the Lower Silesia regional council. Kukiz defined his activity in this institution as social work and not political commitment. He stressed that his council member salary would be given up for charity (Palade, 2015). Kukiz rather skillfully balances on the 'ordinary-special' dimension of the Van Zoonen typology. On one hand, as a popular musician and a celebrity, he was special. On the other hand, both through his style and through the content of his campaign message, he emphasized that he is just an ordinary man leading a typical family life. As an outsider to politics he could be a reliable critic of the political system as a whole.

The outsider persona was not the only dimension of Kukiz' image. An important part of his presidential result was successful activation of the Rebel archetype in his political brand. According to Pearson and Mark, the aspiration of a Rebel is revenge or revolution and his goal is the destruction of that which does not function properly – for the rebel himself or for the entire society (2001, p. 124). The Rebel destroys the existing order, shocks and initiates revolution (2001, p. 124).

The analysis of television advertisements produced by Kukiz and his main opponents, shows that while both Kukiz' contenders decisively advocated the need for stability and security, he was appealing to the need of risk and change – typical of the Rebel. The incumbent president ran his campaign under the slogan: 'Agreement and security'. His rhetoric pointed to the threats to security and stability, which the election of his main opponent could potentially evoke.

In his advertisements Komorowski attempted to activate the archetype of the Ruler who protects from chaos throughout his reign in power (Pearson & Mark, 2001, p. 245) and whose goal is making life as predictable and stable as possible (2001, p. 206). Andrzej Duda with his slogan "A dignified life in secure Poland" was also addressing the need for security in his advertisements. Though, unlike Komorowski, he emphasized that the role of the President is also to take care of the weaker segments of society. A significant aspect of Duda's political spots was the history of poverty-stricken parents who were helped out by the L&J candidate in their conflict with heartless judges trying to take away their children. The spots of the L&J candidate abounded with the announcements of assistance grants to senior citizens and of earlier retirement age to be reinstated. Duda thus, tried to activate the archetype of the Caregiver who "anticipates the needs and reacts in such a way, so that the people may feel safe and taken care of" (2001, p. 207).

In Pearson and Mark's scheme Rebel is in direct opposition to the stability and security embodied by the King. The stage persona of expressive vocalist who assaulted both the left and the right wing of the political scene through his songs combined with the anti-systemic 'particracy' frame locates Kukiz in the niche reserved for the Rebel archetype. The Rebel is an appropriate identity of brand when its consumers feel disaffiliated from the society and identify themselves with the values, which are in contradiction to those of the majority of society. It is also evoked when a function of the product is to destroy something or else when the product itself is authentically a revolutionary one (2001, p. 139).

In line with the predictions of the twelve archetypes, messages of the Rebel in particular appeal to young people entering adult life who are alienated from the dominant culture (2001, p. 128). The poll research data indicates that the most distinctive feature of the Kukiz' electorate was age. In the Presidential election predominantly he got the votes of the young people. In the 18-24 age group he got 46% votes, more than any of his opponents (Boguszewski, 2015, p. 1-2). Almost 80% of Kukiz' election voters voted for Bronisław Komorowski in 2010. Apart from the age similarity, Kukiz voters had in common a more pronounced (than in the case of the electorates of Kukiz 'competitors) criticism of the country's political situation and the most pessimistic evaluation of future perspectives (Boguszewski, 2015, p. 3-4). In the ideological sphere Kukiz' presidential electorate distinguished itself through its conviction of the necessity for protecting existing workplaces and for supporting employment security. This result can be explained by the fact that the youngest segments of the electorate are most threatened by the risk and effects of precarisation (Standing, 2011). Kukiz' electorate did not constitute an ideologically homogeneous group and it is hard to name any major ideological values binding that group together (2015, p.15).

Back to the Roots – Re–authentication Strategy

The relationship between the celebrity persona, message and the needs for a substantial part of the electorate explains the presidential success of Kukiz. How to explain the downfall of the popularity of the 'Kukiz '15 Movement' and its defeat in the September referendum on the voting reform, which Kukiz advocated? In the presidential election, three million people voted in favor of Kukiz, while his flagship referendum issue (i.e. single seat constituency) was supported by only somewhat more than 1.8 million voters (Państwowa Komisja Wyborcza, 2015b).

The reasons for the decline in popularity of the 'Kukiz'15 Movement' may also be perceived in the distinct structure and dynamics of the parliamentary election in which, for instance, the personality of a given candidate seems to be of smaller significance than in the case of the presidential election. In our analysis, we shall focus on the factors to do with the relationship between Kukiz's persona, his message and authenticity. From this perspective it can be stated that 'Kukiz'15 Movement' had become a victim of the successful message of its leader. The Presidential election result of Kukiz meant that he became a part of the world of media and politics. The rock man started to appear more and more in the same mainstream media and amongst the same mainstream politicians, whom he has so fiercely criticized. By crossing the border between celebrity-candidate and celebrity-political organizer he lost the status of an outsider, which was one of the main sources of his authenticity and political capital. His decision to set up a political organization, which seemed a logical outcome of election success, further undermined Kukiz' outsider status. Although Kukiz described his organization as a grassroots social movement and not a classical party, the distinction was not clearly perceived by political commentators or voters. Rather in establishing a party, Kukiz fueled unending media speculation on the candidate lists; connections of the MP candidates of his Movement; his campaign strategy; and future post-election coalitions. In the voters' eyes 'Kukiz' 15 Movement' ceased to differ from standard parties. Kukiz political activity no longer seemed different from the party politics he previously criticized. Thus, Kukiz ceased to be a reliable communicator of his own message. The synergy between his Rebel persona and the framework of socio-political reality, which was used to create his authenticity, stopped working. A signal of crisis was the referendum failure in September.

Faced with the risk of popularity downfall of 'Kukiz' 15 Movement' below the 5% electoral threshold, Kukiz applied three strategies of rhetoric reframing of his own participation in politics in the parliamentary campaign. Since their main objective was to regain authenticity, they can be described as the re–authentication strategy.

Failure of the idea of single seat constituency forced Kukiz to broaden the diagnostic frame of his movement by encompassing the ambition to reform the entire political system. In order to avoid association with standard parties Kukiz stressed that the programme of his movement should be described as a strategy – meaning the focus is not on ruling but on accomplishing the assumed reform. In an emotional style typical of him, he commented on an article in which the political platform of his movement was called 'programme': "STRATEGY!!! Not 'a programme'. 'Programme' is being realized by the party cliques for the last 25 years. Programme of devouring taxpayers' money by means of lies known as promises" (Kukiz, 2015a).

Secondly, in order to defend the integrity of his diagnostic frame and in order to cut away from particracy, Kukiz very strongly emphasized the distinction of his political movement from classical political parties. In this case it was not only a rhetorical frame. The legal status of the Kukiz' organization had significant financial consequences. In Poland, the parties, which enjoy a result over a specific electoral threshold, get subsidies from the state budget. On Facebook, Kukiz (2015b) threatened lawsuits against those who attempted to label his organization a party: "I address the media and 'experts' – political scientists, who in public stubbornly call our organization a PARTY. KUKIZ' 15 IS NOT A PARTY! KUKIZ '15 is a Civic Movement!"

The most important resource Kukiz exploited in his re-authentication strategy was his celebrity persona. This 'comeback to the roots' was especially visible in election spots where Kukiz emphasized his own rock and scenic stage roots (see Fig. 2). In television spots during presidential campaigns his "personal front" (Goffman, 1956, p. 14) consisted of a grey jacket and a shirt unbuttoned at the top. In the parliamentary campaign Kukiz' image is provided with an abundant arsenal of semantic markers signaling his stage and rock, anti-systemic past. In the background, one can see a percussion, floodlights, a microphone. Kukiz wears Doc Martens boots and is in black, the only white element being the national eagle emblem on his t-shirt. In other moments of the advertisement, Kukiz is shown at election campaign meetings singing the movement's election anthem, 'Poland awakens with our dreams', assisted by a rock band. All this seems to serve to convince the voters that he is still Kukiz the rock man, an outsider; the rebel who leads the cohorts to smash down the old system and bring power back to the ordinary people.

Fig. 2. Re-authentication strategy in TV advertisements: left Kukiz "ordinary citizen" in presidential elections (May 2015), right Kukiz "rebel rock man" in parliamentary campaign (October 2015)

Conclusion

The analysis of the Kukiz case shows an important paradox. One of the main arguments of the criticism of the celebrities entering political roles is their lack of political expertise for running important public functions confirmed by achievements and experience. Cultural pessimism, which was already present in Boorstin's opposition of celebrity versus hero, is still strong in the public discourse on the political role of celebrities. In Polish public discourse the word 'celebrity' in relation to 'politician' functions as an insulting epithet. A transformation of persona from the world of pop culture into politics usually requires a rather lengthy 'quarantine' at the lower steps of the political ladder and the leaving aside of some dimensions of the celebrity image. The political career of Ronald Reagan is an example of this very trajectory. In the case of Kukiz, that process has been reversed. Kukiz' image becoming political and losing celebrity-outsider status made him lose his authenticity and undermined his integrity as a communicator of his anti-establishment message. The very thing, which usually is the weakness of a celebrity-politician, in the case of Kukiz, was his key advantage. Hence, he enacted a visible 'back-to-roots' strategy.

The case of Paweł Kukiz shows that in politics, a celebrity can take advantage of his natural characteristic of being a focal point of attention for targeting and steering the emotions of vast numbers of people or else, redirecting these emotions into a political action (voting). As Tyler Cowen (2000, p. 17) observes, celebrities coordinate the activities of large social groups through the simplification of their own image. Kukiz won a relatively big support, as he was the spokesperson of the emotions of a large part of society. Negative emotions in the appraisal of political and economic situation can unite easily. The prognostic frame (voting system reform) of Kukiz failed somewhat short of that success story. For the voters it was just a façade, a pretext for the common expression of negative feelings and a cue of Kukiz authenticity. Hence, the poor result obtained at the referendum. The incumbent President made the same mistake in thinking that the element uniting the Kukiz' voters together was a prognostic frame and not Kukiz as a voice of mass emotions. The announcement of the referendum on single–member districts to win the Kukiz supporters thus, turned out to be an erroneous tactic. Kukiz' supporters were not rejecting the proportional electoral system but, the political status quo in general as represented by the incumbent. The announcement of the referendum seemed to Kukiz' voters as yet another political stunt and reinforced the sense of the incumbent's lack of authenticity. In the second round, 60% of Kukiz' supporters voted for Andrzej Duda and Komorowski lost his reelection bid (Gazeta.pl, 2015).

The novelty of the Kukiz case is the broadening of the standard taxonomy of political celebrities. Kukiz is a rare, if not unique, example of a celebrity creating his own political movement. A single case, and a relatively recent one, is not enough evidence for evaluating the strengths and weaknesses of celebrity-political organizers and for evaluating the effects of the involvement of famous people in such roles. In the very example of Kukiz it seems that the same traits of celebrity persona, which contributed to his success in the Presidential elections, could hamper his functioning behind the scene in the organizational sphere of party politics. Success in the celebrity market or even relative success as a celebrity-candidate requires different competences and character traits than the role of an organizer.

A rare occurrence of a celebrity-organizer in politics may also be influenced by systemic-political factors. American or British party systems based on single seat constituency, of which Kukiz is a fan, usually absorb celebrities (as Ronald Reagan or else, recently Donald Trump) into the structures of existing party organizations. At the same time – according to Duverger's law – in such systems, the celebrity candidate has a small chance of constructing a successful alternative political movement (Duverger, 1975, p. 23-32). Paradoxically, it seems that the political system, which Kukiz criticized for taking the passive voting away from the citizens, has enabled him to effectively construct his own political movement, which has attained a relatively good result in the parliamentary elections.

In context of Donald Trump's win in the US presidential election, the unexpected success of Kukiz and his movement seems to be a part of a larger trend. Professional politics in democracies become boring but most importantly inauthentic. Practices of compromise seem to fail in the place where emotional vision and coherent story count. Therefore, politically inappropriate celebrities from outside the political sphere – like Kukiz, Trump or radical politicians in Europe – seem to be more authentic, closer to the people and more consistent. They function as heroes of certain stories not as cogs in the democratic mechanism of negotiations and compromises. No scandal sticks to them as long as they seem authentic.

References

Benford, R. D., & Snow, D. A. (2016). Framing processes and social movements: An overview and assessment. *Annual Review of Sociology*, *26*(2000), 611–639.

Boguszewski, R. (2015). Kim są wyborcy Pawła Kukiza? *Komunikat Z Badań CBOS*, (86), 1–15.

Cowen, T. (2000). *What price fame?* Cambridge: Harvard University Press.

Duverger, M. (1972). *Party politics and pressure groups; a comparative introduction.* New York: Crowell.

Gazeta.pl. (2015). Wybory prezydenckie 2015. Na kogo głosował elektorat Kukiza? Sondaże nie pozostawiają złudzeń. Retrieved from http://wiadomosci.gazeta.pl/wiadomosci/1,143907,17977416,Wybory_prezydencki e_2015__Na_kogo_glosowal_elektorat.html

Goffman, E. (1975). The presentation of self in everyday life. *Life as Theater*, Edinburgh: University of Edinburgh.

Kukiz, P. (2015a). Strategia!!! nie program. Retrieved from https://www.facebook.com/kukizpawel/posts/966224606778593

Kukiz, P. (2015b). Zwracam się do mediów. Retrieved from https://www.facebook.com/kukizpawel/photos/a.774610832606639.1073741831.7 73389822728740/976720245729029/?type=3&theater

Kukiz, P. (2015c). "(...) bez radykalnej zmiany ustroju... Retrieved from https://www.facebook.com/kukizpawel/posts/958873617513692

Kukiz, P. (2015d). Żenująca jest ta polska scena polityczna. Retrieved from https://www.facebook.com/kukizpawel/posts/958873617513692

Kukiz, P. (2015e). Od 26 lat Polska jest drenowana z kapitału... Retrieved from https://www.facebook.com/kukizpawel/photos/a.774610832606639.1073741831.7 73389822728740/922532651147789/?type=3&permPage=1

Kukiz, P. (2015f). Drodzy przyjaciele!... Retrieved from https://www.facebook.com/kukizpawel/posts/899717266762661

Marsh, D., 't Hart, P., & Tindall, K. (2010). Celebrity Politics: The Politics of the Late Modernity? *Political Studies Review, 8*, 322-340.

Olczyk, T. (2009). Politrozrywka i popperswazja: reklama telewizyjna w polskich kampaniach wyborczych XXI wieku. Warszawa: Wydawnictwa Akademickie i Profesjonalne.

Palade, M. (2015). *Kukiz: król chaosu.* Available from https://www.inbook.pl/p/s/811698/ebooki/literatura-faktu/kukiz-krol-chaosu.

Państwowa Komisja Wyborcza. (2015a). *Wybory Prezydenta Rzeczypospolitej Polskiej 2015. prezydent2015.pkw.gov.pl.* Retrieved from http://prezydent2015.pkw.gov.pl/319_Polska.

Państwowa Komisja Wyborcza. (2015b). *Referendum Ogólnokrajowe 6 września 2015. referendum2015.pkw.gov.pl.* Retrieved from http://referendum2015.pkw.gov.pl.

Państwowa Komisja Wyborcza. (2015c). *Wybory do Sejmu i Senatu Rzeczypospolitej Polskiej 2015.* Retrieved from http://parlament2015.pkw.gov.pl.

Pearson, C. S., & Mark, M. (2001). *The hero and the outlaw. Building extraordinay brands through power of archetypes.* New York: McGraw-Hil.

Popkin, S. L. (1994). *The reasoning voter: communication and persuasion in presidential campaigns* (2nd ed.). Chicago: University of Chicago Press.

Standing, G. (2011). *The precariat: the new dangerous class.* London ; New York: Bloomsbury Academic.

Stankiewicz, A. (2015). *Kukiz. Grajek który został graczem.* Warszawa: Wydawnictwo Fabuła Fraza. Available from https://www.inbook.pl/p/s/795505/ksiazki/reportaze/kukiz-grajek-ktory-zostal-graczem.

Street, J. (2004). Celebrity politicians: Popular culture and political representation. *British Journal of Politics & International Relations*, (6), 435–452.

Trippi, J. (2004). The revolution will not be televised: democracy, the Internet, and the overthrow of everything (1st ed). New York: ReganBooks.

Wasilewski, J. (2012). *Opowieści o Polsce: retoryka narracji.* Warszawa: Studio Headmade.

Zoonen, L. van. (2005). *Entertaining the citizen: when politics and popular culture converge.* Lanham: Rowman & Littlefield Publishers, Inc.

Part III:
Facing Feminism

Having a Driving License in the Movie Theatre: Driver Nebahat

Nilay Ulusoy

Abstract. Yeşilçam Cinema refers to a specific period within the Turkish film industry spanning from the 1950s to the 1970s. During the early Yeşilçam period, the female star Sezer Sezin's on-screen persona of a working-class character, coupled with her off-screen image as a 'tomboy' figure, helped her to become the ultimate movie icon of her generation. Her persona was solidified in the movie *Şoför Nebahat* (*Driver Nebahat*) in 1960, where she played a female taxi driver. During the 1960s, during Yeşilçam's golden years, Sezin's successor Fatma Girik became the new tough, street girl of Turkish cinema. Known for her spirited personality, Girik was a leading lady in Yeşilçam cinema for more than 30 years. In 1970, she filmed the remake of *Driver Nebahat*, where she also played the title character. This chapter will investigate the two different performances in *Driver Nebahat* from Yeşilçam's tough girls in Turkey. During the 1960s, rapid urbanization and the migration flow from rural areas to the industrial cities, that started in the 1950s, seriously accelerated the transformation of the structure of Turkish society, as well as, the position of women in society after the foundation of Turkish Republic in 1923. The aim of this chapter is to analyze Driver Nebahat as a female character and show how it reflected the position of women in Turkey during the golden years of classical Turkish cinema.

Keywords: Turkish cinema, cross-dresser, stardom

Introduction

A star is a reflection of the society from which s/he emerges. The popularity of the on-screen personas of Sezer Sezin (1929 –), one of the first female leads of Yeşilçam Cinema and her successor Fatma Girik (1942 –), and the Driver Nebahat character created in line with their personas, emphasizes various sensitive areas in the 1960s era in Turkey. Although not expressly revealed, the masculine costume pieces worn by Sezer Sezin and later by Fatma Girik in *Driver Nebahat* represent the desire of a young girl, who had undertaken a job as a taxi driver in order to provide for her family following the demise of her father and to temporarily assume the role of a male protagonist. The costume itself, was very well-known to audiences. Since women seldom engaged in work outside the home and in public life. in the melodrama, Driver Nebahat emerges as an interesting character. Roland Barthes suggested that costume supports the main text as a part of the mise-en-scène. Costumes thus form an important component in the analysis of popular culture texts. Additionally, women often pay attention to costumes as a site of pleasure. In the social context of the films the costumes of Driver Nebahat, and the subverted gender roles they symbolize, become significant. This chapter will explore how the progressiveness of popular culture is better understood, through redemptive reading of progressive aspects of the text, and analysis of characters from different points of view (Brunsdon, 1989, p. 121). Briefly, Nebahat's cross-dressing opens a new window into the narrative of melodrama (Ekins & King, 1998, p. 3). Although strong female characters who fought side-by-side with men have been dealt with in numerous films made in the early republican era that depicted the Independence War, Nebahat's masculine outfits and attitudes were also shaping new needs and desires which belonged to the 1950s and 1960s.

According to Ien Ang, female viewing pleasures are the product of women's everyday experience. While female spectators watch melodramas, they can lose themselves in these texts because these cultural products symbolize a structure of feeling, which resonates with how they encounter life (1996, p. 83). In her masculine appearance, Nebahat is a character who alleviated the shock caused by the changes in women's status in terms of jobs, education and active participation in public life that started from the republican reforms of the 1920s. Moreover, she became a role model for the Turkish female spectator – to adapt themselves to modern and working life. Jackie Stacey states that female viewers form an active and direct identification with the stars in two ways. They adore and worship (identificatory fantasies) movie stars while watching films and after the experience of watching them, they interpret them and imitate them in real-life (identificatory practices) (1994, p. 171). Sezer Sezin and Fatma Girik, who played the role of Nebahat, are role models who facilitated women, migrating to big cities from rural areas due to industrialization, to adjust to work in other areas besides agriculture. Therefore, this chapter also considers the on- and off-screen personas of these two renowned stars.

Early Republican Cinema and Comrade Women

Founded in 1923, the Turkish Republic was the first Muslim country to grant political, legal and social rights to women in the first half of the 20th century. The elite who founded the Republic were influenced by nation state ideology, which is a by-product of modern developments (Tekeli, 1999, p. 30). The state positioned women as individuals, who were in charge of founding the new nation state and defined as the most significant symbol of the republic's Westernization and modernization efforts (Göle, 2004, p. 100). A group of women from high socioeconomic backgrounds emerged as pioneers in the Republic and became known as 'comrade women'.

In the early years of the Turkish Republic (1923–1950) movie going experience developed as an urban, upper-middle class habit. These movies were in a way mythological films adopted from early republican literature. Deniz Kandiyoti proposes that female characters from early republican literature were adapted in films of the era and constructed around nationalist ideals. These characters were portrayed as overcoming their individual desires and sexualities, constituting a framework in which women's newly-given civil rights would be used in line with Turkey's founding process as a nation state. The female protagonist, not only chaste but also described as almost sexless, was allowed to co-exist with men in public life as a good productive comrade of the new Republic. She embraces her duties with her plain, functional and masculine clothes. The more she is sexually repressed, the more she feels comfortable in public life. The films made in that era based on popular nationalism aimed to direct audiences towards a cultural and political goal. As virtuous, hardworking and honest people who are in love with only one man, these characters represent the ideal of the comrade women. The Driver Nebahat character, who sacrificed her sexuality, had its beginnings in the narratives of the early republican period. Nebahat is a continuation of a desexualized comrade woman that we find within Yeşilçam Cinema (Kandiyoti, 2007).

The Rise of Yeşilçam Cinema

Filmmaking in Turkey remained limited in scope until the end of the Second World War. When the Republication People's Party (RPP) was shut down by the Democratic Party (DP) in 1950, cinema in Turkey was primarily based on the consumption of mostly American imported films. Having undergone its golden years during the 1960s and 1970s with popular narratives and its power to influence audiences, Yeşilçam's foundations were laid in the 1950s. As more cinema halls opened in various parts of the country and the outskirts of major cities, the film-viewing experience transformed from an expensive, Western-style entertainment to a relatively cheap public spectacle (Arslan, 2011). With the alleviation of the economic depression caused by WW2 and the liberal policies of the DP a positive increase was witnessed in cinema audiences nationwide. The phenomenon of migration from the countryside to the cities caused by the American Marshall Plan to support automation in agriculture as well as construction of new intercity highways that connected Turkish towns, transformed daily life in villages, small towns and major cities. The masses which were affected by rapid population increases in cities, along with urbanization, industrialization, unemployment and inflation. Cinema became the only medium of cheap entertainment (Büker, 2002, p. 165).

This rapid transformation in Turkey's social fabric once again changed the position of women within society. Durakbaşa and Ilyasoğlu suggest that women who participated in public life after receiving an education and having professions were significantly different in terms of class. These women were mostly members of either half-aristocratic or middle-class families that had started to emerge during the early republican period (2001, p. 196). In the 1950s men and women who settled in big cities, coming from different social and economic classes following migration, started to work together in non-agricultural sectors. In Turkey, particularly starting from the 1950s, the rate of working women increased as the industrialization process developed. During the planned development period, which began in 1963, women moved from the agricultural to industrial work force as a result migration to the cities (Doğan, 2013, p. 217). Women attempted to participate in work life to gain economic independence and this led to a shift in traditional gender roles (Kaplan, 2004, p. 33).

Yeşilçam audiences were mostly composed of women from different classes. Female melodramas were an important category within Yeşilçam Cinema and it targeted women as an audience. These films often revolve around traditional realism, with stories of love and family issues. Therefore, female protagonists are at the center of Yeşilçam melodramas (Hollows, 2000, p. 12). Yeşilçam women strive to maintain a balance in their lives in the face of urbanization, modernization and Westernization. In these narratives, where the happiness of the female protagonist hangs by a thread, creating a morally-dignified character with a rich emotional world are key elements (Akbulut, 2008, p. 61). In *Driver Nebahat,* the protagonist, as a beautiful woman, faces many adversities in the profession. Furthermore, she is condemned in the neighborhood and her family is cast out. The business owner from whom they borrowed the car hits on her. In order to cope with all of this, Nebahat starts to wear masculine clothes and embraces a tough attitude. Nebahat, the 'good girl', thus manages to earn her living and bring 'bread to the table' by challenging all the 'bad guys' who try to stop her from 'working with dignity'. In short, Nebahat needs to sacrifice her sexuality in order to work. This was the duty of the aforementioned stars to convincingly play such masculine, yet selfless, and motherly characters.

As a structure that aimed to produce as many films as possible within a short period of time, Yeşilçam produced genre films that capitalized on the star vehicle of actors such as Sezer Sezin and Fatma Girik. Richard Dyer proposed that the star image is a complex composition of visual and verbal, as well as, other different cultural beliefs and perspectives. Therefore, even though stars emerge as characters where gender values clash, they form a common taste for an audience as an experience to end social conflicts (Dyer, 1979, p. 38). Sezin and Girik were two stars loved by the Turkish public. Their portrayal of the

Nebahat character resonated beyond the screen. In the narrative the character was employed in a challenging occupation such as driving. During this period of time (1950s onwards) women from all classes began working. As such the actors' portrayal made the image of a woman who works as a driver outside her home more understandable both to female and male viewers. In particular, in additional to being a well admired female actor, Sezer Sezin was seen as an actress who revealed her femininity in realistic female role, as she often played woman displaying gender confusion. Fatma Girik was also associated with working-class female roles[1] (Özgüç, 2008).

The star image supports the film's narrative and even gives the audience preliminary insight into the film's genre and topic. Regardless of the role the star plays, the different components of the film support his/her image. Barry King proposes that the star's identity is the composition of character traits attributed to the star by the public and his/her character within film (Feasey, 2004, p. 199). Sezer Sezin and Fatma Girik were stars who carried their film personas beyond their roles. Therefore, they matched the public's perception of the masculine-woman prototype, as well as, continuing to play similar characters in other films (Özgüç, 2008, p. 47). The image and attitude of both stars allowed them to be embraced by audiences as cross-dressers.

Yeşilçam's Working-Class Heroine

The starting point of the film *Driver Nebahat* is the demise of the father who represented patriarchal authority. Under these circumstances, Nebahat temporarily grasps power until a new patriarch figure is found. Her sexuality, same as former comrade woman characters in Turkish films, is controlled by patriarchal authority. Despite the fact that the female character represents modern women with her portrayal in Yeşilçam melodramas, the story actually represents a return to traditional values. Women can only be equal to men as long as she dresses like them since it would be impossible to have what is normally considered a man's job (Biryıldız, 1993, p.9). The film does not actually break from existing policies of sexual discrimination and the patriarchal system but, on the contrary, supports it. Cross-dressing gives Nebahat the ability to earn a living by working as a driver. In return, however, Nebahat accepts all the restrictions on her womanhood and strives to prove throughout the film that she fits the male characters' desires. In order to become masculine, Nebahat illustrates how a man is supposed to behave in an

---

[1] Fatma Girik's nickname 'male Fatma-erkek Fatma' is still used in casual language to define tomboyish women. This nickname does not mean to be totally unfeminine but only honest and brave 'like a man' (Dönmez-Colin, 2004, p. 36).

exaggerated manner, one that embodies the male-non-male contradiction. She uses masculine outfits to act freely in society and enjoy certain liberties normally only available to men. The audience, on the other hand, knows this process is temporary and Nebahat will give up cross-dressing once she achieves her goal. The fact that the main goal of the cross-dresser here is to overcome financial hardship is underlined throughout the film (Bruzzi, 1997, p. 151).

Nebahat embraces a masculine attitude and wears men's clothes within the boundaries society has set for her. Her only objective in dressing like a man is to hide her sexual identity. When the lead-male character, Bulent, proposes to Nebahat, she no longer poses a threat to male-dominated society. Nebahat achieves her objective and abandons her masculine identity when Bulent proposes to her in admiration of her courage. Nebahat and her family, in other words, the women and children who lost their father figure, find a new protective male figure. The lead female, in turn, returns home and order is once again restored to comfort the viewer. The savior male figure shows that the film is actually male-centered even though the lead character is a woman. The theme reinforces patriarchy and ensures that women participate in the social order when the ideal family is re-established (Akbulut, 2008, p. 61). The marriage of love, glorified in Yeşilçam films, in fact aims to satisfy many desires felt by female audiences in their daily lives, such as a desire for love or freedom. However, most films ending with a marriage are more likely about a restoration of order rather than the voluntary coming together of two free individuals. It is particularly important for the female lead to abandon her career for the sake of marriage (Kılıçbay& İncirlioğlu, 2003, p. 248). Nebahat will only drive her car for her own pleasure once she gets behind the wheel in her wedding gown.

Movies with female protagonists can privilege a female point of view to solve or diminish contradictions faced by women within a patriarchy. These movies offer women a sense of the problems that patriarchy produces for them, when these movies address both male and female audience (Hollows, 2000, p. 52). Major social transformation followed by cultural change and homogenization are conveyed to the public not only through radical messages but also through the products of popular culture. From this perspective, Nebahat's character fits both the 'masculine woman' and 'girly girl' stereotypes dictated by Yeşilçam Cinema (Biryıldız, 1993, p. 9). At the same time, however, when Nebahat makes a living from driving a car, this is seen as a man's job. It can also be seen as an indication of the change in women's position in society during the 1950s and 1960s. *Driver Nebahat* is an early example of the notion that women can succeed in existing and adapting to the world of men.

Nebahat as an Ideal Heroine

For female audiences, as pointed out above, a heroine is an ideal they identify with. This reveals audience's desires that are suppressed in daily life. For male audiences, however, she is an object of desire glorified by the use of all elements of a patriarchal society (Gledhill, 1991, p. 87). Moreover, the Driver Nebahat character, as a cross-dresser, manages to combine these qualities in the eyes of the viewer, both as a source of authority (male) and an object of desire. Nebahat's character allows the female viewer to act freely and participate in life while finding romantic love. The male viewer sees the attractive heroine as an object of desire even though she looks and acts like a man. For these reasons, Nebahat's character is doubly an object of desire. We watch Nebahat's transformation in the film through her reflection in the mirror. She lifts her shirt-collar up and tucks her hair in her cap. We can see from her looks that she is fully self-confident. When spying on Nebahat in the rearview mirror, as Laura Mulvey put it, both female and male audiences embrace a patriarchal perspective by objectifying the female character (Smelik, 1998, p. 5). Even though Nebahat adopts a masculine look, she is positioned as an object of desire in the film as she continues to be worth looking at. This goes on throughout the entire film. The camera focuses on Nebahat in scenes where Nebahat looks at herself through the mirror or sits in the driver seat. While Nebahat watches customers sitting in the backseat, the reflection of her face in the rearview mirror is always in focus.

However, with a female character who can do both, they also allow male viewers to form a bisexual identification with the character (McCabe, 2004, p. 42). Highlighting biological sex hidden under masculine clothes with a feminine detail is a method used by cross-dressers (Bruzzi, 1997, p. 177). Nebahat's hair protruding from underneath her cap underlines her femininity. This is one of the most important details as it reminds the audience that she is actually a woman. Flügel proposes that those who wear phallic clothes, smoke cigarettes and use phallic accessories, such as a walking stick, aim to express themselves comfortably in public. Use of these symbols show the desire to gain the same public status and power as men in public life (Flügel, 2008, p. 128). Nebahat, wearing her cap, lighting her cigarette and wearing a leather jacket can confidently work as a driver.

Since phallic symbols are a proud exhibition of masculine power, loss of the same represents castration (Flügel, 2008, p. 129). Nebahat, seen wearing a shirtwaist dress and high-heeled shoes while at home, suggests that a woman actually belongs at home. When Bülent is proposing to her, Nebahat is dressed in light colored clothes; she has taken off her hat, which cast a shadow to her face; and her hair is down. Dresses, wool fabric and light-colored clothes are feminine symbols according to Freud (2001 [1963], p. 158). When Nebahat takes off her masculine clothes, it means that she is giving up her masculine identity. She becomes a woman again once she stops wearing phallic symbols. With holy matrimony, the male object castrates the masculine woman and destroys her masculine features. However, despite her masculine appearance, Nebahat as a character, who can exist in men's world and finds true love and on whom 'a wedding gown looks beautiful', appears as a protagonist that in particular female viewers can identify with.

Car as a Symbol of Femininity

According to Flügel, clothes are shields that protect us from the outside world once we leave our mothers' wombs. Wearing clothes outside replaces the protective environment of the home. Furthermore, like boats, buckets and homes, cars also represent the womb as a feminine symbol (Flügel, 2008, p. 127). For the identities of those who drive them, cars serve as symbols. The interiors, seats and lights of cars help to identify it with home – the only difference being they do not belong to a certain location. Cars are actually moving homes, which transport the driver to a certain place (Orr, 1993, p. 165). According to Parla, on the other hand, a car is a symbol of modernization in Turkey, and provided a safe passage between the privacy of the home and the public aspect of the street. This feature of cars is used to reflect characters as an extension of real-life in cultural products (2003, p. 548). Nebahat leaves home, drives all day and goes back home. Actually, in this respect, she is never outside of her home. Nebahat's car is both a workplace and an object of her desire. Her reason for working as a driver is to make the car's installment payments so she can own it. Her car is her protector and she is also responsible for everyone who gets into it. She leaves the hospital in her wedding gown on Bulent's arm and gets into her car. She drives Bulent in her car to the place where they are supposed to get married. Nebahat drives home in her car, which she will only drive for her family from now on. The movie explicitly orients the female audience to 'direct their hearts to hearth and home' by promoting 'romantic love and marriage' at the end of the movie. However, regardless of whether it is a horse, or a car, Riding/Driving is a tour de force, which hints at "a superiority achieved against those who are left on the ground" (Ergüven, 2000, p. 136). The experience of driving can also be an experience with which "a person can increase his power ... through a capsule resembling the womb in which he is by himself in various ways without having relationships with others. The person's power can increase by slightly pushing the gas pedal" (Freund-Martin, 2000, p. 130–131). Nebahat, who does not even leave the steering wheel of her car to Bülent, is a character of power in a setting where she feels safe by protecting herself from others outside.

Conclusion

Deniz Kandiyoti suggested that drawing a comparison between the feminist movement in Western societies and the process of modernization and enlightenment processes of women in the Muslim World is 'oversimplification'. According to Kandiyoti, a male dominant system has both protective and suppressing properties whereas women have their own resources of power and independence (Kandiyoti, 1987, p. 334). As stated earlier, women's rights which were used as a tool to modernize the society during the early years of the Republic has led to a 'modern yet modest' comrade women character. Although Nebahat could be identified as a comrade woman, she is also a courageous character who pushed the boundaries of the traditional fabric of Turkish society and took a step further by wearing masculine clothes instead of plain ones. Moreover, different from early republican upper middle class comrade women, she became a role model for others. Nebahat, is a character who chose to get a job in order to stand on her own feet and challenged the system on her own, thus her liberated herself by way of cross-dressing in order not to be exploited.

Christine Gledhill argues that cultural forms are both a product and source of 'cultural negotiations', an ongoing process of cultural exchange (1988, p. 67). Turkish audiences recognized Turkey's rapid change in cinema, which was also happening all around them. They felt the change in values that was occurring due to increased consumption, urbanization and Westernization. The female audience wanted to balance this reshaping world with the traditional values they relied upon. As Yeşilçam melodramas attempted to achieve a compromise between tradition and modernity, the audiences themselves imagined cooperation with the stars. Audiences' intimate connection with Sezin and Girik are reminiscent of the sincere relationship among the lower-class characters in films, and of the supposed social relationships among the members of a traditional neighborhood.

Genres such as melodramas aimed directly at female audiences are constituted primarily through the culturally constructed skills of femininity – sensitivity, perception, intuition and the necessary privileging of the concerns of the personal life (Brunsdon, 1981, p. 32). However, even though Nebahat seems like a character who complies with patriarchal rules, she is also a protagonist who displays unique and courageous behaviors. Firstly, she appears as a character who decides to be self-sustained and implements her decision with courage and shows initiative. She is brave; she is not deterred by her neighbors, or men who molest her while she is working. She succeeds in being a driver, which is an occupation that requires attention, coolness and technical skills and thus seen fit for men. At the end of the film, she drives the wedding car herself and does not let the groom take the wheel. Actually, this suggests that Nebahat will take the control of her marriage. The popularity of the Nebahat character paved the way for two sequels respectively titled *Nebahat the Driver and Her Daughter* (1964), and *Nebahat, We Are Offender* (1965), as well as a remake of the first movie (Scognamillo, 1998, p. 320). While the film reflected how social gender relations had been constructed during the modernization period; it also featured clashes between modern social norms and resistant traditional ones, as well as, the struggle of women to emerge as an individual during such struggle. It can be said that Nebahat was a reflection of the female workforce in Turkish cinema, which increased by 5.8% within the decade following the year 1960 during which a planned economy policy was implemented by the state (Küçükkalay, 1998, p. 41). In the film, women's participation in the work force has only been visually demonstrated while the character has not been marginalized. Therefore, the film did not depict modern social gender roles as a phenomenon, which de-womanized women but merely demonstrated the society's traditional segment's acceptance and tolerance of modern values. In fact, the name 'Nebahat the Driver' was established in Turkish as an idiom and has become a widely used description for women who drive well and who are honest and hard-working.

References

Akbulut, H. (2008). *Kadına Melodram Yakışır: Türk Melodram Sinemasında Kadın İmgeleri, [Melodrama Befitting to Woman: Female Images in Turkish Melodramas]*. Istanbul: Bağlam.

Ang, I. (1996). *Watching Dallas: Soap Opera and the Melodramatic Imagination.* London, New York: Routledge.

Arslan, S. (2011). *Cinema in Turkey: New Critical History.* Oxford, New York: Oxford University Press.

Biryıldız, E. (1993). Şoför Nebahat mı olalım, Küçük Hanımefendi mi? [Do We Have to be Driver Nebahat or a Little Lady?], *Journal of Marmara İletişim. 4*, 1-14.

Brunsdon, C. (1981). Crossroads: Notes on Soap Opera, *Screen, 22*(4), 32-37.

Brunsdon, C. (1989). Text and Audience, In E. Seiter, H. Borchers, G. Kreutzner &E.m. Qarth (Eds.), *Remote Control: Television, Audiences and Cultural Power* (pp. 116-129). London, New York: Routledge.

Bruzzi, S. (1997), *Undressing Cinema: Clothing and Identity in the Movies.* London, New York: Routledge.

Büker S. (2002). Film Baştan çıkarıcı bir öpüşmeyle bitmiyordu, *Kültür Fragmanları:Türkiye'de Günlük Hayat*, [The Film Does Not End with a Seductive

Kiss], In D. Kandiyoti&A. Saktanber (Eds). (Zeynep Yelçe Trans.) *Cultural Fragments: Casual Life in Turkey* (pp. 159-182). Istanbul: Metis.

Doğan, M. (2013). A General Outlook on the Industrialization Process of Turkey, *Journal of Marmara Geography*, *28*, 211-231.

Dönmez-Colin, G. (2004). *Women, Islam, and Cinema.* London: Reaktion Books.

Durakbaşa, A & İlyasoğlu, A. (2001). Formation of Gender Identities in Republican Turkey and Women's Narratives as Transmitters of 'Herstory' of Modernisation, *Journal of Social History. 35*(1), 195-203.

Dyer, R. (1979). *Stars.* London: British Film Institute.

Ekins, R. & King, D. (1998). *Blending Genders: Social Aspects of Cross-Dressing and Social Change.* London: Routledge.

Ergüven, M. (2000). Çağdaş Kentauros, *Cogito: Otomobil Özel Sayısı,* [Contemporary Centaur, *Cogito: Automobile Special Edition*], *24*, 133-138.

Feasey, R. (2004). Stardom and Sharon Stone: Power as Masquerade, *Quarterly Review of Film and Video*, *21*(3), 199-207.

Flügel, J. C. (2008). Giysi Sembolizmi ve Giysinin Çok Anlamlılığı,İnsan Giyinir ['Symbolism and the Multiple Meaning of Clothes', Human Dress], *Cogito*, 55, 121-132.

Freud, S. (2001, [1963]). *(1915-1916) Introductory Lectures on Psycho-Analysis (Parts I and II), (Vol. XV)* (2001 ed.). A. Freud, & J. Strachey (Eds. Trans.). London: Vintage Books.

2015, June 16). Symbolism in the Dream, *A General Introduction to Psychoanalysis.* Retrieved from: http://www.bartleby.com/283/10.html

Gledhill, C. (1991). *Stardom: Industry of Desire.* London, New York: Routledge.

Göle, N. (2004). *Modern Mahrem: Medeniyet ve Örtünme [The Forbidden Modern: Civilization and Veiling].* Istanbul: Metis.

Hollows, J. (2000). *Feminism, Femininity, and Popular Culture.* Manchester, New York: Manchester University Press.

Kandiyoti, D. (1987). Emancipated but Unliberated? Reflections on the Turkish Case, *Feminist Studies*, *13*(2), 317-338

Kandiyoti, D. (2007). *Cariyeler, Bacılar, Yurttaşlar: Kimlikler ve Toplumsal Dönüşümler,* [Odalisques, Sisters, Citizens: Identities and Social Transformations] A. Bora, F. Sayılan, Ş. Tekeli, H. Tapınç & F. Özbay (trans.) 2nd Edn. Istanbul: Metis.

Kaplan, N. (2004). *Aile Sineması Yılları 1960'lar [Family Cinema Years, The 1960s].* Istanbul: Es.

Kılıçbay, B. & Onaran İncirlioğlu, E. (2003). Interrupted Happiness: Class Boundaries in Turkish Melodrama, *Ephemera: Critical Dialogues on Organization*, *3*(3), 236-249.

Küçükkalay, A.M. (2011). Türkiye'de Planlı Dönemde Kadın Nüfusu ve Kadın İşgücü İstihdamındaki Gelişmeler [Developments in Female Workforce and Population in Planned Economy Period in Turkey] *Journal of Suleyman Demirel University Faculty of Economic and Administrative Sciences, 3*, 35-44.

McCabe, J. (2004). *Feminist Film Studies: Writing the Woman into Cinema.* London, New York: Wallflower.

Orr, J. (1998). *Sinema ve Modernlik* [*Cinema and Modernity*], (A. Bahçıvan Trans.). Ankara: Ark.

Özgüç, A. (2008). *Türk Sineması'nın Kadınları,* [*Women of Turkish Cinema*]. Istanbul: Agora.

Özön, N. (2013). *Türk Sineması Tarihi: 1896-1960, [History of Turkish Cinema: 1896-1960].* 4th Edn. Istanbul: Doruk.

Parla J. (2003). Car Narratives: A Subgenre in Turkish Novel Writing, *The South Atlantic Quarterly*, *102*, 535-550.

Scognamillo, G. (1998). *Türk Sinema Tarihi, [History of Turkish Cinema].* İstanbul: Kabalcı.

Smelik, A. (1998). *Feminist Sinema ve Film Teorisi: Ve Ayna Çatladı, [Feminist Cinema and Film Theory: And the Mirror Is Cracked]* (Deniz Koç. Trans). Istanbul: Agora.

Stacey, J. (1994). *Star Gazing: Hollywood and Female Spectatorship.* London, New York: Routledge.

Tekeli, İ. (1999). Değişenin Değiştirme Zorunluluğu Var mı?. 75 Yılda Değişen Yaşam Değişen İnsan ve Cumhuriyet Modaları, [Transformation Has the Reason to Transform?, *Republican Fashion and Transformation of People and Life in 75 Years*]. In. O. Baydar & D. Ozkan (Eds.), (pp.131-132). Tarih Vakfı Yayınları: İstanbul.

Celebrities and Conflicting Notions of Modern Feminist Embodiment

Kelly M. O'Donnell

Abstract. This chapter looks at how celebrity feminists are shaping the understanding of feminism in 2016. Emma Watson and Miley Cyrus are self-identified feminists who advocate differing feminisms. Availability heuristics is used to examine the barriers that preclude full acceptance of free choice feminist embodiment; and the ways in which the feminist status quo is maintained. Cyrus's free choice feminism challenges and is challenged by availability heuristics of feminist embodiment. Watson's feminist work fails to challenge the patriarchy or address the underlying causes of inequality. The two women are contrasted to illustrate differing conceptions of feminist enactment. Media coverage of the two women illustrates how society's availability heuristics about feminist embodiment are conceived and reified. The virgin/whore paradigm is at the heart of the fight over feminist embodiment.

Keywords: Celebrity feminism, Miley Cyrus, Emma Watson, availability heuristics

Introduction

The media play an important role in making what was once on the fringe or taboo, into something mainstream. The "continuous interactions" that women and young people have with entertainment news and with each other "shape[s] our [their] perspectives and orientation toward reality" (Vavrus, 2002, p. 3). The American Press Institute (2014) found that 58% of 18-29-year olds and 46% of 30-39-year olds follow entertainment news. This is a significant number of people consuming entertainment news, so what is reported and *how* it is reported is increasingly important. Much of the entertainment news that is consumed by Americans is found online through social media, especially on Facebook, a platform that 64% of adults in the U.S. use and 73% of the news they see is about entertainment (Anderson and Caumont, 2014). These "continuous interactions" give an incredible amount of power to self-identified feminist celebrities (Vavrus, 2002).

However, feminists must always walk a delicate line in the fight to take the feminist project to the next level—full acceptance and equality on women's terms. The line is between the self-actualized feminist (whore) and the undemanding social conformist (virgin). The conception of feminists is still ruled by antiquated myths and tropes of bra burning man haters. Only 20% of

Americans identify themselves as feminists according to a 2013 poll, and more men and women thought that the term feminist had a negative connotation (Swanson, 2013). Celebrity women who fall on either side of the line face their own set of challenges and do their work under a microscope. This chapter puts that microscope on Emma Watson and Miley Cyrus, but not for clicks or shares, but to atomize what works and what is problematic about each woman's brand of feminism, utilizing the virgin/whore paradigm.

Women are still sexualized in their media representations, whether it is by their own will or the will of their handlers and feminist scholars still argue over sexualization (Attwood, 2007). Lerum and Dworkin (2009) challenge the problematic notion that sexualization is inherently negative, by noting that the concept: does not take into account a woman's ability to analyze the commercialization of her body and make her own decisions about it, that "false" hegemonically driven "dichotomies…focus only on constraining aspects of sexuality" (p. 255), and that it fails to explore "connections between sexualization and power" (p. 256).

Slut-shaming is at the core of arguments over sexualization. Armstrong, Hamilton, Armstrong and Seeley (2014) argue that women who call each other sluts or engage in slut-shaming are a product of class relations. Slut-shaming "is about drawing class-based moral boundaries…women's definitions of sluttiness revolve around status…which is largely dictated by class" (E.A Armstrong, Hamilton, E.M. Armstrong, & Seeley, 2014, p. 101). Miley Cyrus is the daughter of a country singer from Tennessee. Southerners are often labeled "white trash" and "rednecks" whether they are or not. The term supposes that poor white people from the south and other rural areas have no pedigree or power to speak of and are "others" who do not embody desirable qualities of race or socioeconomic status (Wilson, 2002). Richard Cohen (2013) called Cyrus, "a cheap act, no doubt about it" and "a tasteless twit". The self-sexualization of Cyrus is automatically viewed as trashy and slutty, a distinction which is arbitrary and based on classist tropes.

Availability Heuristics

Kahneman (2011) discusses what he terms "availability heuristics" as the ability of a person to recall a large number of pieces of information that answer a question and make a decision based on those pieces of information. The tropes surrounding feminism are small pieces of information that require very little effort to recall numerous instances where one may have encountered a person who embodied that trope. The "ugly, angry, lesbian feminist" is a trope that is easy to access. For instance, Rosie O'Donnell has often been characterized this way, yet the reason for her alleged anger requires more thought and reasoning than can be accessed as easily as the stereotype. Celebrity culture has great power and the misunderstandings that are perpetuated by women in public fail to challenge the patriarchal underpinnings on which these heuristic beliefs are based.

Celebrities are brands; they endorse products, have their own lines of beauty products, and are themselves commodities traded on the open market be it in album sales, television shows or movies. The importance of celebrity influence on the heuristic understanding of feminism cannot be understated. Zeisler (2016) recounts numerous examples of celebrities relying on antiquated and damaging tropes when they were asked about their connection to feminism. Evangeline Lilly stated:

> I'm very proud of being a woman, and as a woman, I don't even like the word feminism because when I hear that word, I associate it with women trying to pretend to be men, and I'm not interested in trying to pretend to be a man. (Zeisler, 2016, loc. 2072)

Lilly's understanding of feminism is based on the availability heuristic of damaging tropes and discourses that rely on "the importance of an idea" which is "often judged by...[the emotional charge) with which that idea comes to mind" (Kahneman, 2011, p. 142). Lilly's celebrity status gives power to this flawed understanding of feminism and increases the availability heuristic of her fans, which acts to perpetuate tropes surrounding feminism and feminists.

The Feminist Brand

Emma Watson—the virginal Hermione Granger, the good girl, the smart girl, the woman parents want their daughters to grow up emulating; is the kind of feminist our foremothers envisioned. Miley Cyrus—the once beloved Hannah Montana, the naked twerking whore, the gender queer omnisexual, is the last woman parents want their daughters emulating, in fact, "78% of British parents don't want children to be influenced by Miley Cyrus" (Morgan, 2015). Both of these women are self-identified feminists, and they are both problematic. Watson is problematic for the new generation of feminists and Cyrus is problematic for the second wave feminists who feel they still get to define what it means to be a feminist in 2016. By analyzing the 'virgin' Emma Watson and the 'whore' Miley Cyrus a grey area emerges for both women in terms of their sexualization, but more importantly how it ties to their 'versions' of feminism.

Women who self-identify as feminists have the ability to change the discourse by taking responsibility for the public face of feminism and dispelling untruths and harmful ever-persistent tropes. At the core of the debate around women is the discourse of the virgin/whore paradigm. These two discourses form different aspects of the overarching discourse of feminist celebrity women. This overarching discourse is the idea that beautiful virginal white women are the only appropriate women to promote the feminist project. Zeisler (2016) addresses the media's declaration that Emma Watson was a bigger feminist than Beyoncé, stating:

> In a competition that no one had asked for, corporate media outlets seemed to breathe a collective sigh of relief, as though finally, finally [emphasis in original], there was a straightforwardly appropriate celebrity vessel to express exactly the right amount of feminism in exactly the right way, with no complicating factors like scanty stage wear. (Chapter 5, Section 2, para. 20)

It is not just corporate media who breathed a sigh of relief when Emma Watson declared herself a feminist. Our second wave foremothers flocked to her, both Gloria Steinem and bell hooks granted Watson interviews in a clear endorsement of her brand. Watson was also chosen to be a UN Goodwill ambassador and started the #HeForShe campaign, while simultaneously taking her project global, interviewing Malala Yousafzai (Watson, 2015) and author Marjane Satrapi (Vogue, 2016). Watson took time off from acting to pursue study of feminism and promote her version of global feminism.

Watson's brand is not just the 'beautiful white virginal woman', her public persona is equated with that of the character who made her famous, Hermione Granger.[1] Her "multi-year contract with the Harry Potter franchise ensures that her fans will know her as Hermione" (Sweeney, 2008, p. 8). Watson herself stated, "I feel as though I spent a long time trying to pretend I was not like Hermione. And of course, I was rather like Hermione" (Satlin, 2016). By being inextricably linked to Hermione Granger, she has a large body of work, which reinforces her brand as the smart, rule following, and purely good character seemingly reflected by off-screen actions.

Miley Cyrus's brand, since her departure from Disney, is quite different than Watson's. Cyrus wears next to nothing on stage and poses in nothing at all in photo shoots and her music videos. The public's disdain for her hyper-sexualization is rooted in her label as the wanton whore. In 2013, after her MTV VMA performance with Robin Thicke, the Parents Television Council, of which her father is a board member, asked MTV to "keep the 2014 ceremony clean" (Weingarten, Shipley, Fischer & Johnston, 2013). Cyrus's interviews are laden with profanities and her stage performances include a number of sexual fetishes, which play into her image.

---

[1] Watson appeared as the studious Hermione Granger in the *Harry Potter* film franchise.

In 2013, Cyrus said, "I feel like one of the biggest feminists in the world because I tell women not to be scared of anything" (Izundu & Butterly, 2013). The brand of feminism that Cyrus self-identifies with is marked by the free choice promoted by the individualism of third and fourth wave feminism. Zaslow (2009) argues, "for sex-positive feminists, media texts that depict women embracing sexual desire and playing with sexuality may be powerful because they challenge traditional representations of women as passive objects rather than active subjects in the hetero-sexual encounter" (p. 62). Cyrus's sexual public persona provides this challenge through her self-assertion that she is in fact a feminist despite her outfits or lack thereof. Cyrus's embodiment of a feminist, in her own words, is a project to allow "girls to be free with their sexuality…I'm a part of the evolution of that. I hope" (Gevinson, 2014).

Cyrus states that her over the top persona is meant to wake them up, to save them from the perils of teenage conformity (Farrow, 2014). "I'm trying to tell girls, like, fuck that. You don't have to wear makeup. You don't have to have long blonde hair and big titties [sic]. That's not what it's about. It's about, like, personal style" (Farrow, 2014). A critical look at Cyrus's feminism places it within a nuanced understanding of the term. The freedom of choice that she advocates has long been a tenet of feminism, so why do her critics rely on the second wave discourse that removes sexuality from feminism? Attwood (2007) argues it is because, "an earlier women's movement saw as a key source of women's oppression…struggles over sluttiness have become more politically charged… and in the last ten years they have also become a part of a struggle over feminism itself" (p. 243). Feminist embodiment discourses threaten feminism itself if we do not start to argue for a broader understanding of feminism and feminists themselves.

O'Connor v. Cyrus

Miley Cyrus found herself in the crosshairs of Sinead O'Connor in 2013, after her MTV VMA performance with Robin Thicke, dubbed "The twerk seen round the world" (Weingarten, et al, 2013) and Cyrus's statement that her *Wrecking Ball* video was inspired by O'Connor's *Nothing Compares to You* video (Brady, 2015). Brady highlights feminist commentary that contextualizes "the Cyrus/O'Connor 'feud' within wider debates over sexual agency, 'celebrity feminism' and contemporary media culture" (p. 430). O'Connor penned an open letter to Cyrus, stating:

> Nothing but harm will come in the long run, from allowing yourself to be exploited, and it is absolutely NOT in ANY way an empowerment of yourself or any other young women to send across the message that you

are to be valued (even by you) more for your sexual appeal than your obvious talent [emphasis in original].

As Brady observes, central to the exchange and accompanying media commentary "are determinations of what counts as feminist action, and who gets to adjudicate on its political veracity" (p. 432). Richard Cohen (2013), a 75-year-old white man, conflated Cyrus with the Steubenville rape case, suggesting her performance had "set the women's movement back on its heels", two charges that take a woman's embodiment out of her hands without her permission or agreement.

Musician Amanda Palmer (2013) challenged O'Connor's stance in an open letter, which advocated for the free choice of third wave feminism. Writing about the double bind that women find themselves in, she states, "It's a Chinese finger trap that reflects the basic problems of our women-times: we're either scolded for looking sexy or we're scolded for not playing the game" (Palmer, 2013). Palmer (2013) goes on to encourage O'Connor to create a space where artists and all other women could freely express themselves in any way they chose. Gay (2014) concurs, stating, "it's quite the contradiction to want to overthrow the patriarchy but also to believe that, even now, the patriarchy is so omnipotent that women are incapable of making empowered decisions when they make decisions that don't tow the feminist party line". The idea that women can control their own sexualization or be sexualized at all without causing harm to the feminist project is still contested, and will remain so until more women embrace both or allow each other the space to do so.

Watson's Problematic #HeForShe

When Emma Watson was made a UN Goodwill Ambassador in 2014, she delivered a speech about feminism and launched her #HeForShe campaign. The speech was lauded as "game-changing" by *Vanity Fair* (Robinson, 2014) and other media outlets, earning her a spot on *Time Magazine's* 100 most influential people in 2015 (Abramson, 2015). Watson's UN speech was problematic in that she focused on "white feminism", "first world problems", and heteronormative binary conceptions of women and men (McCarthy, 2014). However, her impact on raising the profile of feminism is undeniable. As Robinson notes, Watson represented "a rare case where an actor being conflated with their role might be a good thing." In particular, Watson is more influential for the relatively younger *Harry Potter* audience who are "… (still forming their opinions on gender roles and advocacy) … than other high-profile defenders of the F-word" (2014). Watson offers an alternative image of 'feminist', previously used by the media "to describe hairy-legged stereotypes" (McCarthy 2014). She is, in McCarthy's words "a newer, hipper, prettier feminism based entirely on an 11-minute speech at the United Nations" (2014). #HeForShe has been endorsed by many celebrities and fans, but a closer look at her remarks is warranted.

The premise for the #HeForShe campaign is, "how can we affect change in the world if only half of it is invited or feel welcome to participate in the conversation?" (Watson, 2014). She goes on to "extend [men their] formal invitation" to join feminism (Watson, 2014). She asserts that the project should be about giving men the opportunity and freedom to be sensitive fathers so that women will finally be valued. Feminism can and does incorporate the struggles of everyone who is oppressed, however to liken the struggle of men to that of women negates a millennium of struggle for rights and privileges that were ordained to men in law and through social constructions of the roles of men and women.

Watson started a feminist book club called 'Our Shared Shelf', which boasts 160,000 members. She also has taken to leaving the book club's picks in London subways (WITW Staff, 2016). These actions make for good news stories, but as McCarthy (2014) argues, #HeForShe like so many other hashtag campaigns lacks any practical use beyond a selfie with a whiteboard emblazoned with the hashtag. Watson does not propose any solutions in her speech, and while reading feminist books is enlightening for many, it does not equate to action in the real world.

During a Twitter Q&A, Watson had to answer for claims that she is a "white feminist" as a result of her UN speech, stating that she "wants to hear as many voices as possible" (Blay, 2015). She did not propose ways of accomplishing this, or expand on the matter. The coverage of her UN speech and her Twitter Q&A gave her a pass on her lack of nuance, allowing that at least she is trying (Blay, 2015). Meanwhile *Seventeen* and *Teen Vogue* covers fawned over her responses; "Emma Watson's empowering Twitter Q&A is all the advice you will ever need," lauded *Seventeen* (Bruk, 2015). My argument here contrasts Watson with Cyrus, in that Cyrus does not align herself with a movement, but instead values individual expression of feminism and Watson identifies herself with a movement, but outlines no action beyond reading a book. The difference between the power feminism of Cyrus and the liberal feminism of Watson is often reduced to a conversation about the former's sartorial choices and the latter's legitimacy as a UN Goodwill ambassador.

Gay (2014b) interestingly foreshadowed Watson's speech, stating, just two months before Watson's UN speech:

> Recently, a young woman asked me how we can make feminism more accessible to men. I told her that I don't care about making feminism more

accessible to men. In truth, I don't care about making feminism more accessible to anyone. (Gay, 2014b)

The point that she is making is one that is lost in discussions of feminist celebrities. Gay (2014b) notes that celebrities are gateways for other women to learn about feminism, but if women only focus on the words coming out of the mouths of Jennifer Lawrence or Emma Watson, then they are not digging deeper into the institutionalized and structured ways in which women are oppressed. Enck (2014) argues that everyone can "create change through sustained critique and tropological deconstruction" and can "alter the microlevel and macrolevel systems in which they live (p. 203). Both Watson and Cyrus can take on the role of educator through their status as celebrities and go beyond the actions and words they have thus far taken to challenge these larger structures and oppressive institutions.

Conclusion

Celebrities have a platform that can be used for both good and ill. We read about them with alacrity and morbid fascination. However, the proliferation of online media allows us just enough time to look at what celebrities say and make a snap judgement. Celebrities can open the door, but it is academics who must break down the door, the wall and all the windows in the room. Watson and Cyrus can simultaneously "value individual experience as epistemic" while also "situating these truths within larger power structures" to give not just a voice to feminist activism, but to empower women's truth (Enck, 2014, p. 202-203).

Miley Cyrus has received criticism for her onstage persona and her claim of feminism. What is often left out of these critiques is that women should be able to express themselves in whichever way suits them. The individual empowerment strategy of Cyrus challenges the protectionism of the prevailing patriarchal (and second wave feminist) dictates of women's embodiment. Cyrus could raise her credibility by framing the issue in a more articulate manner, utilizing critical pedagogical tools for connecting personal action, thereby fighting socio-cultural constructions, which ignore her message.

Watson, on the other hand has taken the feminist project to a larger audience. What is problematic about her work is that it is based on the idea that feminist's work thus far has eluded the goal of gender equality by not incorporating men into the conversation. Women's truths will elude men until they enter the mainstream consciousness through enactment that challenges heuristic beliefs about women and feminists. Her scholarship, #HeForShe campaign, and book club do not propose any real action beyond quiet micro-level projects done at home or in the virtual world of hashtags and Tweets.

Well-intentioned projects and public statements by celebrities are a step in the right direction, but we do ourselves a disservice by not demanding more of them. Few people have the kind of access that Watson and Cyrus have, few command their level of devoted attention by millions of fans, and few have the opportunity of using that platform to make a real difference. Critical pedagogues, activists, academics, and teachers can join the conversation and elevate the discourse beyond good-feminist / bad-feminist dichotomies by jumping on the celebrity bandwagon and correcting what needs correcting, and praising what deserves praise.

References

Abramson, J. (2015, April 27). Emma Watson. *Time, 185*(15,16), p. 55.

American Press Institute (2014, March 17). Social and Demographic differences in news habits. *The American Press Institute Online*. Retrieved from https://www.americanpressinstitute.org /publications/reports/survey-research/social-demographic-differences-news-habits-attitudes/

Anderson, M. & Caumont, A. (2014, September 24). How social media is reshaping news. *Pew Research Center*. Retrieved from http://www.pewresearch.org/fact-tank/2014/09/24/how-social-media-is-reshaping-news/

Armstrong, E.A., Hamilton, L.T., Armstrong E.M., & Seeley, J.L. (2014). "Good girls": Gender, social class, and slut discourse on campus. *Social Psychology Quarterly, 77*(2), 100-122.

Attwood, F. (2007). *Mainstreaming sex: The sexualization of western culture.* London: Touris.

Baumgartner, J. (2011*). F'em! Googoo, Gaga, and some thoughts on balls*. New York, NY: Seal Press.

Blay, Z. (2015, October 15). Emma Watson gives smart answer when asked if she is a 'white feminist'. *Huffingtonpost.com*. Retrieved from http://www.huffingtonpost.com/entry/emma-watson-gives-smart-answer-when-asked-if-shes-a-white-feminist_us_561bea68e4b0dbb8000f4ea9

Brady, A. (2016). Taking time between g-string changes to educate ourselves: Sinead O'Connor, Miley Cyrus, and celebrity feminism. *Feminist Media Studies, 16*(3), 429-444.

Bruk, D. (2015, January 28). Emma Watson's empowering #HeForShe Twitter Q&A is all the advice you will ever need. *Seventeen Online*. Retrieved from http://www.seventeen.com/celebrity/q-and-a/a26570/emma-watson-twitter-qa-gender-equality/

Cohen, R. (2013, September 2). Richard Cohen: Miley Cyrus, Steubenville and culture run amok. *TheWashington Posat Online.* Retrieved from https://www.washingtonpost.com/opinions/richard-cohen-miley-cyrus-steubenville-and-culture-run-amok/2013/09/02/1cecafa6-11af-11e3-bdf6-e4fc677d94a1_story.html

Enck, S. (2014). Feminist communication activism pedagogy— "gender and violence: Dominance, resistacne, and the cultural production of meaning". In Frey, L.R. & Palmer, D. L. (Eds.), *Teaching communication activism: Communication education for social justice.* New York, NY: Hampton Press, Inc.

Erchull, M.J. & Liss, M. (2013). Feminists who flaunt it: exploring the enjoyment of sexualization among young feminist women. *Journal of Applied Social Psychology*, 43, 2341-2349

Farrow, R. (2014, February 3). My oh Miley! *W Magazine Online.* Retrieved from http://www.wmagazine.com/story/miley-cyrus-ronan-farrow.

Foucault, M. (1978). *The History of sexuality: Volume 1: An introduction.* New York, NY: Pantheon Books.

Foucault, M. (1980). Two lectures (C. Gordon, L. Marshall, J. Mepham & K. Soper, Trans.). In Gordon, C. (Ed.) *Power/knowledge: Selected interviews and other writings 1972-1977* (pp. 78-108). New York, NY: Pantheon Books.

Gay, R. (2014a, May 12). Beyonce's control of her own image belies the bell   hooks 'slave' critique. *The Guardian Online.* Retrieved from http://www.theguardian.com/commentisfree/2014/may/12/beyonce-bell-hooks-slave-terrorist.

Gevinson, T. (2014, April 30). Not a girl not yet a woman: The two sides of Miley Cyrus. *Elle online.* Retrieved from http://elle.com.culture/celebrities/a12/miley-cyrus-may-cover-story.

Howard, H. (2015, October 14). Emma Watson is not a white feminist. *Teen Vogue Online.* Retrieved from http://www.teenvogue.com/story/emma-watson-white-feminism-twitter-chat.

Izundu, C. & Butterly, A. (2013, November 12). Miley Cyrus says she's 'one of the biggest feminists'. *BBC Online.* Retrieved from http://www.bbc.co.uk/newsbeat/article/24911610/miley-cyrus-says-shes-one-of-the-biggest-feminists.

Kahneman, D. (2011*). Thinking, fast and slow*. New York, NY: Farrar, Straus and Giroux.

Lerum, K. & Dworkin, S.L. (2009). "Bad girls rule": An interdisciplinary feminist commentary on the report of the APA Task Force on the Sexualization of Girls. *Journal of Sex Research*, 46(4), 250-263

McCarthy, A. (2014, September 26). Sorry privileged white ladies, but Emma Watson isn't a 'game changer' for feminism. *Huffington Post*. Retrieved from http://www.huffingtonpost.com/xojane-/emma-watson-feminism_b_5884246.html.

Morgan, M. (2015, August 25). Parents rank Miley Cyrus as the WORST celebrity role model for children…while the Duchess of Cambridge is named the best. *The Daily Mail Online*. Retrieved from http://www.dailymail.co.uk/femail/article-3209970/Parents-rank- Miley-Cyrus-WORST-celebrity-role-model-children.html.

O'Connor, S. (2013, October 3). Sinead O'Connor's open letter to Miley Cyrus. *The Guardian online*. Retrieved from http://www.theguardian.com/music/2013/october3/sinead-o-connor-open-letter-miley-cyrus.

Palmer, A. (2013, October 6). An open letter to Sinead O'Connor, Re: Miley Cyrus. [Blog] *Blog.AmandaPalmer.net*. Retrieved from http://www.blog.amandapalmer.net/ 20131003

Robinson, J. (2014, September 21). Watch Emma Watson deliver a game-changing speech on feminism for the U.N. (Updated). *Vanity Fair Online*. Retrieved from http://www.vanityfair.com/hollywood/ 2014/09/emma-watson-un-speech-feminism

Satlin, A.H. (2016, Febraury 25). Emma Watson tells Gloria Steinem how she's like Hermione in feminist chat of our dreams. *HuffingtonPost.com*. Retrieved from http://www.huffingtonpost.com/entry/emma-watson-gloria-steinem-have-feminist-chat-of-our-dreams_us_56cf14d5e4b03260bf759a88.

Swanson, E. (2013, April 16). Poll: Few identify as feminists, but most believe in equality of sexes. *Huffington Post*. Retrieved from http://www.huffingtonpost.com/2013/04/16/feminism-poll_n_3094917.html.

Sweeney, K. (2008). *Maiden USA: Girl icons come of age*. New York, NY: Peter Lang.

Vavrus, M.D. (2002). *Postfeminist news: Political women in media culture*. Albany, NY: State University of New York Press.

Watson, E. (2014, December 1). Transcript of Emma Watson's speech on gender equality at the U.N. *About Education online*. Retrieved from http://sociology.about.com/od/Current-Events-in-Sociological-Context/fl/Full-Transcript-of-Emma-Watsons-Speech-on-Gender-Equality-at-the-UN.htm.

Watson, E. (n.d.). *Our shared shelf. GoodReads.com*. Retrieved from https://www.goodreads.com/group/show/179584-our-shared-shelf.

Watson, E. (2015, October 9). Twitter Q&A with Emma Watson. *Twitter*. Retrieved from https://twitter.com/EmmaWatson/status/652539534203207680.

Weingarten, C. R., Shipley, A., Fischer, R. & Johnston, M. (2013, August 23). 32 most outrageous MTV VMA's moments of all time: From Miley's twerk to Eminem being a jerk, the craziest highlights from the ceremony's wild past. *Rolling Stone Online*. Retrieved from http://www.rollingstone.com/music/lists/30-

most-outrageous-mtv-vmas-moments-of-all-time-20140820/miley-cyrus-robin-thicke-and-the-twerk-seen-round-the-world-2013-20140820.

WITW Staff. (2016, November 11). Surprise! Emma Watson leaves copies of   latest book club pick on London subway for lucky readers. *New York Times Online.* Retrieved from http://nytlive.nytimes.com/womenintheworld/2016/11/02/emma-watson-leaves-copies-of-latest-book-club-pick-on-london-subway-for-lucky-commuters/.

Wilson, J.A. (2002). Invisible racism: The language and ontology of 'white trash'. Critique of Anthropology, *22*(4), 987-401.

Zaslow, E. (2009). *Feminism, Inc.: Coming of age in girl power media culture.* New York, NY: Palgrave Connect (Online Service).

Zeisler, A. (2016). *We were feminists once: From Riot Grrrl to Cover girl, the buying and selling of a political movement.* New York, NY: Public Affairs.

Part IV:
Leaving a Legacy

Phoenix Rising: Freddie Mercury's Legacy and the Fight Against AIDS

Marie Josephine Bennett

Abstract. The 1980s saw a rise in diagnoses of HIV/AIDS. One of the earliest high-profile cases of a celebrity contracting AIDS was the American actor Rock Hudson, who died in October 1985. In the UK, Freddie Mercury's death from AIDS-related bronchial pneumonia in November 1991 was much publicized. There had been rumors that Mercury was unwell for some time. As early as 1986, a tabloid newspaper published a story alleging that Mercury was ill, although this suggestion was strenuously denied. Mercury did not reveal that he was dying from an AIDS-related illness until the day before his actual death.

Mercury rose to fame as lead singer of the pop group Queen, and, following his death, the remaining members of the group organized 'The Freddie Mercury Tribute Concert for AIDS Awareness' as a way of celebrating their fellow band member's contribution to popular music, but also to raise money for AIDS' research. The concert took place on 20 April 1992, and was broadcast live on television. The profits were used to launch the Mercury Phoenix Trust, a UK-registered charity, later that year. In this chapter, I show how Mercury's celebrity status has encouraged others to raise money for the Trust, which provides funds to a number of non-governmental organizations worldwide to help try and eradicate HIV/AIDS.

Keywords: AIDS, celebrity, Mercury, Phoenix Trust, Queen

Introduction

Larry Z Leslie (2011) proposes that "Celebrities are one of popular culture's most important products" (p. xiii) and, using well-known pop singer Michael Jackson as his example, argues that, even after somebody famous has died, "a celebrity's reputation and work may live on" (p. 35). As a result of technological advances over the last few decades, it is now simple to access an artist's oeuvre at the touch of a button, and become familiar with the music and songs of stars who have died. As Andy Bennett (2016) suggests, "It is an interesting, not to say sometimes ethereal, experience to watch film and video recordings of deceased rock and pop artists engaging in performances that have now come to be regarded as seminal moments in their respective careers" (p. 61). Indeed, as discussed in this chapter, this is very much the case with regard to the lead singer of the pop group Queen, namely Freddie Mercury, particularly via his performance at the Live Aid concert at Wembley Stadium in 1985, which was widely praised and won the group a number of new admirers. But it was a later concert at the same venue following Mercury's death that was to launch a charity that has become part of the singer's legacy, benefitting many people worldwide in the fight against AIDS.

This chapter outlines why Mercury's continuing popularity and celebrity following his death initiated the foundation of the Mercury Phoenix Trust, an organization that aims to help eradicate HIV and AIDS worldwide. It argues that the singer's talent and star status has enabled the charity to continue to benefit as a result of his renowned musical legacy and fans' fundraising activities, even many years after his death. Furthermore, Mercury's sexual orientation and struggle to maintain his privacy towards the end of his life raised important issues about attitudes towards homosexuality and bisexuality amongst the wider public. His decision not to reveal the cause of his illness until late in the day was eventually respected, given the downside of celebrity for a man who wished to retain his privacy for as long as possible.

As well as, providing some background information about Mercury, the band Queen, and their rise to fame, the chapter suggests that two televised performances in particular gained the group a strong fan base and admiration for their talents, especially those of Mercury. It examines the ways in which the media investigated and reported on the singer's changed appearance and eventual admission that he had contracted AIDS. Additionally, it also evaluates the ways in which Mercury's celebrity, fandom and sexual orientation led to the founding of the charity set up in his name.

Background

Freddie Mercury was born Farrokh Bulsara in Zanzibar in September 1946; his parents were from Gujarat, India. He moved to England with his parents and younger sister in 1964. Mercury met guitarist Brian May and drummer Roger Taylor through mutual friends and together they formed the band Queen in 1970, with long-term bassist John Deacon joining the group the following year. They achieved chart success in the UK in 1974 following the release of their second and third singles, 'Seven Seas of Rhye' and 'Killer Queen'. The chart-topping 'Bohemian Rhapsody' from the album *A Night at the Opera* brought further acclaim in 1975, remaining in the number one position for nine weeks. At the end of their UK tour to promote the album, the group was invited to play a concert at Hammersmith Odeon in London on Christmas Eve of that year, which was broadcast live on both television and radio in the UK. Such was its popularity that the concert was shown again in December 1976 "by public demand" (Gunn & Jenkins, 1992, p. 103). This 'groundbreaking' concert was released on DVD and other formats as 'A Night at the Odeon' in November

2015, an indication of Queen and Mercury's enduring popularity.[1] It was to be another live performance by the group, this time in 1985, which would concretize Mercury's celebrity status, and gain the group – including Mercury – new fans.

Live Aid and Celebrity

Both Ellis Cashmore and Chris Rojek discuss the link between celebrity and talent. Cashmore (2006) suggests that, from the late 1980s, there was a change in the way celebrity was perceived, such that fame and merit were no longer coterminous, and argues that there has been a "shift of emphasis from achievement-based fame to media-driven renown" (p. 7). But he proposes that some celebrities do become well-known as a result of their talents in specific fields, such that "they serve political ends… as well as providing pleasure for the masses" (p. 263). Rojek (2001), meanwhile, distinguishes between three different types of celebrity status, which he terms "*ascribed*, *achieved* and *attributed*" (p. 17).[2] Mercury's celebrity status falls into the second of these, as defined by Rojek; such celebrities "are recognized as individuals who possess rare talents or skills" (p. 18).

The distinctive vocals of lead singer Mercury, his theatrical and energetic style as frontman of Queen when performing live, and his skills as a songwriter, were some of the reasons for the group's worldwide success. The combination of these elements was arguably most acknowledged and admired when the band performed at the Live Aid concert at Wembley Stadium in July 1985. Live Aid was organized by singers Bob Geldof and Midge Ure in order to raise awareness about the plight of those affected by famine in Ethiopia and more importantly to provide much needed funds to help alleviate their suffering.[3] Numerous stars were invited to perform. Greg Brooks notes that the concert was "beamed over satellite to over 160 countries" (p. 217) and suggests that Queen's performance gained them numerous new fans (p. 218). As reported by John Earls (2015), Ure has stated that, during the Queen set, Mercury had "the audience in the palm of his hand" (p. 31).

---

[1] See http://www.queenonline.com/en/news-archive/press-release-a-night-at-the-odeon-to-be-released-on-november-20th/ At the time of writing, two of the group's original members continue to tour under the name Queen, fronted by American singer Adam Lambert.

[2] Italics in original text.

[3] The concert followed on from the release of the charity single 'Do They Know It's Christmas,' written by Geldof and Ure, which was released in December 1984.

David Marshall (1998) states that, fundamental "to the construction of the popular music celebrity is the conveyance of both commitment and difference," (p. 163) with commitment being linked both to the way stars relate to their fans in terms of their authenticity, and how the fans relate to the stars. In some cases, "authenticity is expressed through the performer's communication of solidarity with an audience" (p. 164). It is interesting, therefore, to consider in this respect the crowd's reaction to Mercury's performance at Live Aid as a way of verifying his status as celebrity.

Queen's performance was limited to around 20 minutes in length due to the number of acts appearing. The band decided to play a number of their hits, starting with a section from 'Bohemian Rhapsody,' followed by 'Radio Ga Ga,' a single, which had peaked at number two in the UK charts the previous year. Although partly guided by Mercury, it appears that everyone in the crowd joined together as one, raising their hands in unison to clap throughout the song's chorus.[4] This number was followed by Mercury's acapella 'call and response' section, during which he sang notes to syllables such as 'eh' and 'oh' and waited for the audience to copy him, which they automatically did. During 'Crazy Little Thing called Love,' Mercury stops singing at one point to allow the audience to do so, clapping along with them, and similarly in 'We Will Rock You,' he permits the audience to sing the chorus at times in his stead. Queen's performance at Live Aid, and that of Mercury in particular, can therefore be acknowledged as a good example of a pop star showing solidarity with his audience, and vice versa. This is of particular note given that the unity and camaraderie he created was with an audience comprised of people who were not necessarily Queen fans; rather it was a mixed group gathered to support a cause. This connection with the audience has also been noted by Bennett (2016), who suggests:

> Freddie Mercury's celebrated performance with Queen at Live Aid... has become a historic 'moment' but also, due to the way they have been captured on film and subject to continual replay, they appear to be suspended in time, reaching out to audiences and fuelling their memories... That audiences are able to relate to music icons in this way has much to do with the mode through which such icons are presented to and connect with their audience. (p. 62)

Mercury's mesmerizing live performances and musical talents helped to propel the group – and Mercury in particular – to fame and fortune. Importantly, the

---

[4] Such movements would have been familiar to those acquainted with the promotional video released to accompany the song.

Live Aid concert increased his popularity and celebrity, such that he was a more recognizable figure. Indeed, Matt Richards and Mark Langthorne (2016) argue that the performance "revitalised Queen's fortunes and gave the band a new lease of life" (p. 269). Mercury's early death, and the cause of his death, therefore had a wider impact than would have been the case without Live Aid; his resulting raised profile in turn increased the profile of the issue of AIDS awareness.

Mercury's Sexual Orientation

Even from the group's early days, Mercury was evasive concerning his sexual orientation. Julie Webb, a reporter from music paper *New Musical Express* (*NME*), wrote in April 1974 that, if asked whether or not he was gay, he would simply respond "as a daffodil." In an interview with journalist Caroline Coon (1974) in *Melody Maker* later that year, on being told that he was "on the way to being a huge androgynous sex symbol," Mercury did not claim to be gay or bisexual, merely stating that, "I think mystique, not knowing the truth about someone, is very appealing" (p. 8).

Androgynous appearances by male pop stars during the early part of the 1970s were *de rigueur*, as glam rock was at its peak. Glam was as much a fashion statement as an expression of sexual preference. Male singers and musicians often wore sparkly and colorful outfits, jewelry, make-up, and platform-soled shoes. Philip Auslander (2006) argues that glam rock was more about the way people dressed than style of music, stating that "some glam rockers, notably Bolan, Bowie, and Lou Reed, professed homosexuality or bisexuality," but "most simply adopted glam as a provocative performance style" (p. 41). Thus, Mercury's visual image when the group achieved early chart success – dark eyeliner, black nail varnish and high heels – was nothing out of the ordinary. Indeed, Barney Hoskyns (1998) argues, "no act got away with camp in quite the way that Queen did" (p. 99). At this stage, therefore, Mercury does not seem to have been trying surreptitiously to denote his sexual orientation via his appearance.[5]

There was, however, a noticeable change to Mercury's visual persona in the early 1980s, which hinted at his sexual preferences. Martin P. Levine (1998) has discussed the 'gay clone' look assumed by many homosexual men in the United States around this time. Those who donned this look "kept their hair short, beards and mustaches clipped" (p. 61) and "wore the sturdy, utilitarian

---

[5] Mercury lived with his then girlfriend Mary Austin for some years during the band's early days and the two remained very good friends. See, for example, Jones (1997, p. 8-9).

clothing associated with traditional macho icons" (p. 60). Phil Sutcliffe (2009) observes that in the promotional video for the single 'Play the Game,' released in 1980, Mercury was "wearing the complete '80s macho 'gay clone' look – hair cropped, black moustache, no more nail varnish" (p. 148). Nevertheless, whilst Mercury assumed this look, he was still elusive in public regarding his sexual preferences. Whilst not openly 'coming out' at that time, however, Mercury was engaging in casual relationships with other men, particularly in New York (Jones, 1997, p. 197). In the United States during the early 1980s, New York "accounted for one-half of the nation's AIDS caseload" (Eisenbach, 2006, p. 294); Richards and Langthorne (2016) argue "it is likely" that Mercury contracted HIV while in New York in 1982 (p. 220).

Reporting of Mercury's Illness

The magazine *New York* ran a feature by Edwin Diamond on 2nd March 1987 entitled 'Celebrity Aids.' Within the article, Diamond suggests that "More than any recent breaking news story, the AIDS epidemic has exposed questions of journalistic standards, confidentiality, and privacy" (p. 16). This is interesting, given Mercury's celebrity status and the approach taken by the media in the UK to validate their suspicions that Mercury was seriously ill. As early as 1986, a tabloid newspaper suggested that Mercury had contracted HIV. In an article printed on the 18th of October that year, journalist Hugh Whittow of *The Sun* questioned Mercury at Heathrow Airport regarding blood tests reportedly carried out at a London clinic. Mercury allegedly "turned ashen-faced," but told Whittow that he was "perfectly fit and healthy."

The Sun's headline on 29th April 1991, accompanied by a photograph of the singer, was "Tragic Face of Freddie Mercury." Writer Stephanie Scawen stated in her article that Mercury looked "painfully thin" despite the fact that he denied being unwell. Publishing the same photograph on their front page on 8th November that year, the newspaper's Piers Morgan and Dan Collins reported that an AIDS specialist had been seen visiting Mercury at his home. This information was also front-page news in the *Daily Star* on the same day, accompanied by the disapproving headline, "Why are you hiding, Freddie?" with journalist Virginia Hill again noting that an AIDS specialist had visited the singer. As Mark Blake (2010) explains, "The press were now keeping a permanent vigil outside the house" (p. 353) with "almost fifty journalists and photographers camped outside" (p. 355). Indeed, Richard Smith (2016) argues that Mercury "spent the last weeks of his life being hounded by the press" and suggests; "the fact that he'd died from an AIDS-related illness made the fact of his homosexuality – a subject he himself had always been vague about – unavoidable" (p. 234). Rojek notes celebrity "homosexuality has a long history of being vigorously denied" (2001, p. 86). Arguably, however, Mercury did not so much deny being gay or bisexual as skirt the issue. Yet, such considerations seemed more important to the media than to the fans and did not impact detrimentally upon his celebrity status in the way journalists perhaps thought it might, an important issue given the aims of the charity to which his name would be linked following his death.

Stephen Hinerman (2006), writing about tabloid newspapers in relation to the accusation of child abuse made against Michael Jackson, argues that, "When scandal emerges in the public life of a star, tabloids quickly enter the process" (p. 458). Despite the other members of the band trying to protect their friend, the tabloids were keen to dig deeper, fueled by Mercury's obvious weight loss and lack of visibility in public. Of course, as Hinerman argues, there has to be some truth to rumors about stars for tabloid papers to hope to reveal something scandalous about them (p. 458). However, despite his more reclusive lifestyle and evident gaunt appearance during the televised BRIT awards ceremony[6] in February 1990, Mercury did not reveal publicly that he had been diagnosed with AIDS until 23rd November 1991. In a statement read out by press officer Roxy Meade, the following had been written:

> Following enormous conjecture in the press, I wish to confirm that I have been tested HIV positive and have AIDS. I felt it correct to keep this information private to date to protect the privacy of those around me. However, the time has come now for my friends and fans across the world to know the truth, and I hope that everyone will join with me, my doctors and all those worldwide in the fight against this terrible disease. My privacy has always been very special to me and I am famous for my lack of interviews. Please understand this policy will continue. (cited in Hawkins, 2016, p. 143)

It is interesting how many references there are to privacy in this short statement. However, by this point, Mercury knew he was nearing the end of his life, and this arguably accounted for the timing of the statement to the media; he was too ill to be affected personally by any derogatory comments.

Sadly, Mercury passed away the following day. His death, which was as a result of AIDS-related bronchial pneumonia, was much publicized on television, radio, and in the press. While most reports focused on his musical talents in their tributes, this was not the case in all the obituaries, a number of which revealed homophobic predilections. For example, a column in the *Daily Star* (1991) suggested that the singer was responsible for "pressing his own

---

[6] British Phonographic Industry's annual pop music awards. See also Gunn and Jenkins (1992, p. 236).

self-destruct button" (p. 2). However, Joe Haines's (1991) article in the *Daily Mirror* was probably the most disparaging. Entitled 'Dark Side of Freddie', he stated, "What concerns me today is the example set by Freddie Mercury the man." Claiming that he should have revealed the truth about his illness earlier, Haines continued that, rather than being an idol, the singer "was sheer poison, a man bent... on abnormal sexual pleasures." Furthermore, he proposed, his "private life is a revolting tale of depravity, lust and downright wickedness." Such articles exemplify the difficulties Mercury would have faced if he had revealed his illness to the public when first diagnosed, especially given his celebrity status. Furthermore, the inevitable press interest such a disclosure would have sparked would also have impacted on the other members of Queen, making it extremely problematic for the group to continue recording further albums and singles without intense press intrusion; despite his illness, Mercury was keen to work for as long as he possibly could.

Cashmore (2006) suggests of celebrities that, "we seem to delight in their sense of self-importance, their scandalous behavior, and their eagerness to deplore the media's intrusions" (p. 266). But there was genuine grief following Mercury's death. Fans congregated at his London home to leave letters, flowers and memorabilia outside. Also, the gates of the house were opened a few days after his death so that grieving fans could look at the numerous wreaths that had been sent.[7] Indeed, his fandom and status remains such that mourners still visit. Writing in 1996, Waldemar Januszczak of *The Sunday Times* newspaper observed, his "fans are... reluctant to let him go" (p. 61). Given this suggestion, it is interesting that Bennett (2016) has argued that, rock "stars cast an iconic presence over society, a quality that persists even in death" (p. 61). Mercury was certainly a star and icon for many, and his death led to the foundation of a charity that continues to benefit many people throughout the world. Steve Jones (2005), debating why certain celebrities "live on after death" (p. 270), suggests that, unlike "many, perhaps most, other types of celebrities, musicians seem to fall into a particular category of acquaintance" (p. 271). The "reluctance to let him go" expressed by Januszczak, and the possibility to "live on" as indicated by Jones, come to fruition not just through the ability to still listen to and watch Mercury via modern technology, but also via the charity to which fans and admirers can contribute, such that it has become part of his posthumous legacy.

---

[7] Reported in *The Sun*, 27.11.91

The Mercury Phoenix Trust

Blake (2010) reports that fellow band members May and Taylor "were adamant that Mercury wanted the world to know he had AIDS to raise awareness" (p. 359). However, it is unclear when and how such a conversation took place. Certainly, Mercury liaised with Queen manager Jim Beach just prior to releasing the press statement in which he revealed his illness, and there was general agreement by a number of those close to the singer "that a lot of good could come out of Freddie admitting that he had AIDS while he was still alive" (Richards & Langthorne, 2016, p. 363). It is important, therefore, to separate Mercury's wish for peace and privacy from press intrusion in the last weeks of his life, from the suggestion that he did not want people to know that he had AIDS. It is more likely, given what was said by his bandmates, that he wanted control over when the information about his illness was revealed openly, rather than it being a journalistic 'scoop'.

Following Mercury's death, the single 'Bohemian Rhapsody' was re-released, with all profits from sales donated to the Terrence Higgins Trust, a UK-based AIDS charity.[8] In its February 1992 edition, *Vox* magazine journalist Martin Townsend argued that the singer's "private struggle against AIDS has already changed attitudes towards the disease" (p. 10) and included details about how to make donations to the Terrence Higgins Trust. At the BRIT Awards ceremony in February 1992, at which Mercury posthumously received the award for an Outstanding Contribution to Music, drummer Taylor announced that there would be a concert in honor of Mercury's memory later that year. This was entitled 'The Freddie Mercury Tribute Concert for AIDS Awareness' and provided an opportunity for the other members of the group and fellow musicians not only to pay tribute to the Queen singer, but also to help raise money for AIDS' research. The concert took place at Wembley Stadium before some 72,000 fans on Easter Monday, 20 April 1992, and was broadcast live on television and radio in over 70 countries.[9] Performers included such luminaries as David Bowie, Liza Minnelli, Annie Lennox, George Michael and Elton John. Even then, there was some dissention and cynicism expressed in the press. For example, Paul Mathur (1992), writing in *Melody Maker*, decried the concert as an opportunity to view "all the usual old lags slap each other's backs" rather than to raise awareness about AIDS. He also denounced Mercury as someone "never as stellar as his name" and who "on

---

[8] Higgins was the first person in the country known to have died as a result of developing AIDS.

[9] http://news.bbc.co.uk/onthisday/hi/dates/stories/november/24/newsid_2546000/2546945.stm.

finding he was HIV positive didn't have the courage of character to admit it" (p. 12).

Discussing singer Karen Carpenter and her fight against anorexia nervosa, Peggy J. Bowers and Stephanie Houston Grey (2005) argue that often "for diseases to capture the public imagination, they require a personification" (p. 101). Certainly, the fact that Mercury was a household name was beneficial in highlighting AIDS Awareness. Consequently, the profits from the concert were used to launch the Mercury Phoenix Trust (MPT),[10] a UK-registered AIDS charity, later that year. An EP entitled 'Five Live', featuring two performances from the concert, was released worldwide in 1993 in order to raise money for the Trust.[11] Three years later, an exhibition of photographs of Mercury was held at the Royal Albert Hall in London, before moving to Japan and a number of European cities, thereby making a strong link between Mercury's celebrity status, his fans, the cause of his death, and the aims of the Trust. Although the exhibition was free of charge, memorabilia such as posters and brochures were available for purchase; profits from these sales were again given to the Trust. In 2002, the MPT joined with EMI to release a DVD of the Tribute Concert.

Also a gifted artist – he attended Ealing College of Art in London before joining Queen – Mercury created the 'Queen crest' or logo, which was shown on the group's drum kit in the band's early days, as well as on many album covers. Based on the Royal Coat of Arms of the United Kingdom, the crest features a large letter Q surrounded by figures that represent the four band members via their signs of the zodiac. At the top of the Q is a phoenix, a mythical bird, which in Greek mythology is reborn from the ashes of its predecessor and thus symbolizes immortality.[12] The phoenix was therefore, a fitting symbol for the Trust to employ in order to identify themselves with Mercury and become part of his legacy.

Set up as a memorial to Mercury, the MPT provides funds to a number of non-governmental organizations in a variety of countries to help try and eradicate HIV and AIDS; to date, over 50 countries have received donations from the Trust. Their aim is to "fight AIDS worldwide" and they only donate to HIV- and AIDS-related projects, particularly grassroots organizations. They endeavor in particular to provide funding to projects aimed at children who

---

[10] See http://www.mercuryphoenixtrust.com/.

[11] George Michael, Lisa Stansfield and the remaining members of Queen feature.

[12] The legend of the phoenix is not unique to Greek mythology; it also features in many other cultures and countries, such as Egypt and China. It is possible that Mercury chose this symbol because it is the crest of his old school in India, St Peter's. See http://www.peterspanchgani.org/.

have been orphaned as a result of AIDS. The Trust states, "Help us to use Freddie's memory, his charisma and drive to eradicate this disease,"[13] and there are indeed strong links between the charity and Mercury's fans. This is noted by Harry Doherty (2014), who states that the Trust is boosted by "the continued support of the members of Queen and fans and friends around the world" (p. 95). For example, there is a worldwide event called 'Freddie For A Day' (FFAD) that was launched in September 2010, and which is now held annually near to Mercury's birthday. The aim of participating in the event is to raise awareness and funds by being sponsored to dress up as the singer – or simply to wear a fake moustache. In addition, the Queen Studio Experience, based in Montreux, gives fans the chance to visit the recording studio owned by the group between 1979 and 1996. The exhibition includes photos and memorabilia from Queen's personal archives. Although it is free to visit, any donations from visitors are given to the Trust. As Doherty (2014) explains, whilst progress has been made in the fight against the spread of HIV and AIDS, the funding of projects by the Trust "is still… essential work" (p. 95). As someone who died as a result of contracting HIV/AIDS, it is thus beneficial that Mercury's name is linked to the charity to promote their cause.

Conclusion

Daniel J Boorstin (1961), arguing that the media is responsible for creating celebrities, has stated that a celebrity is somebody "who is known for his well-knownness" (p. 57). However, Mercury's fame resulted from his musical talents as a singer, songwriter and performer. In controlling, via his management, the point at which he disclosed his AIDS' diagnosis, he gained the respect of fans and supporters of those living with HIV and AIDS, while his celebrity helped to bring awareness of the disease into the public domain.

Mercury was just 45 at the time of his death. Rojek (2001) rightly notes that, celebrity "immortality is obviously more readily achieved in the era of mass communications, since film footage and sound recordings preserve the celebrity in the public sphere" (p. 78). As reported by Gunn and Jenkins (1992), in the Fan Club magazine distributed around Christmas 1991, band member May has praised Queen's fans and stated, "Freddie, his music, his dazzling creative energy – those are for ever" (p. 248). Mercury's "celebrity immortality" stems not just from the ability to hear recordings of his songs or relive his performances, but also because his huge and continuing popularity has enabled thousands to benefit as a result of the successful and vibrant charity set up in

---

[13] http://www.mercuryphoenixtrust.com/site/aboutus.

his name which, given its successful appropriation by fans with regard to fund-raising activities, has become a valued component of the Queen singer's enduring legacy.

Acknowledgments

I would like to thank Vicky Vocat of the Mercury Phoenix Trust for checking the information in this chapter relating to the Trust for factual accuracy.

References

Auslander, P. (2006). *Performing Glam Rock: Gender and Theatricality in Popular Music*. Michigan: The University of Michigan Press.

Bennett, A. (2016). Mediation, Generational Memory and the Dead Music Icon. In C. Strong and B. Lebrun (Eds.), *Death and the Rock Star* (pp. 61-72). Abingdon, Oxon, New York, NY: Routledge.

Blake, M. (2010). *Is This the Real Life? The Untold Story of Freddie Mercury & Queen*. Cambridge, MA: Da Capo Press.

Boorstin, D. J. (1961). *The Image: A Guide to Pseudo-events in America*. London: Weidenfeld and Nicolson.

Bowers, P. J. and Houston Grey, S. (2005). Karen: The Hagiographic Impulse in the Public Memory of a Pop Star. In S. Jones and J. Jensen (Eds.), *Afterlife as Afterimage: Understanding Posthumous Fame* (pp. 97-120). New York, NY: Peter Lang Publishing Inc.

Brooks, G. (2005). *Queen Live*. London, New York et al: Omnibus Press.

Cashmore, E. (2006). *Celebrity/Culture*. Abingdon, Oxon: Routledge.

Coon, C. (1974, December 21). Queen Bee. *Melody Maker*, p. 8.

The *Daily Star* Says column. (1991, November 26). Tragic waste of a genius. *Daily Star*, p. 2.

Diamond, E. (1987, March 2). Celebrity Aids. *New York*, pp. 16-20.

Doherty, H. (2014). *The Treasures of Queen*. London: Carlton Books Ltd.

Earls, J. (2015, Aug/Sept). Live Aid. *Classic Pop, 18*, 24-33.

Eisenbach, D. (2006). *Gay Power: An American Revolution*. New York: Carroll and Graf Publishers.

Gunn, J. and Jenkins, J. (1992). *Queen: As It Began*. London, Basingstoke: Sidgwick and Jackson Limited.

Haines, J. (1991, November 28). Dark Side of Freddie. *Daily Mirror*. Retrieved from https://placowkapostepu.files.wordpress.com/2010/04/joe-haines-freddie-mercury.jpg.

Hawkins, S. (2016). *Queerness in Popular Music: Aesthetics, Gender Norms, and Temporality*. New York, Abingdon, Oxon: Routledge.

Hill, V. (1991, November 8). Why are you hiding, Freddie? *Daily Star*, p. 1.

Hinerman, S. (2006). (Don't) Leave Me Alone: Tabloid narrative and the Michael Jackson child-abuse scandal. In P. David Marshall (Ed.), *The Celebrity Culture Reader* (pp. 454-469). New York, Abingdon, Oxon: Routledge.

Hoskyns, B. (1998). *Glam! Bowie, Bolan and the Glitter Rock Revolution*. London: Faber and Faber.

Januszczak, W. (1996, November 17). Star of India, *The Sunday Times Magazine*, pp. 51-64.

Jones, L. (1997). *Freddie Mercury: The Definitive Biography*. London: Hodder and Stoughton.

Jones, S. (2005). Echo Homo. In S. Jones and J. Jensen (Eds.), *Afterlife as Afterimage: Understanding Posthumous Fame* (pp. 269-276). New York, NY: Peter Lang Publishing Inc.

Leslie, L. Z. (2011). *Celebrity in the 21st Century: A Reference Handbook*. Santa Barbara, California: ABC-CLIO.

Levine, M. P. (1998). *Gay Macho: The Life and Death of the Homosexual Clone*. New York, London: New York University Press.

Marshall, P. D. (1998). *Celebrity and Power: Fame in Contemporary Culture*. Minneapolis, MN: University of Minnesota Press.

Mathur, P. (1992, May 2). It's, Uh, Kinda Tragic. *Melody Maker*, p. 12.

The Mercury Phoenix Trust – About Us. Retrieved from http://www.mercuryphoenixtrust.com/site/aboutus.

Morgan, P. and Collins, D. (1991, November 8). Top AIDS docs see Freddie Mercury. *The Sun*, p. 1.

Richards, M. and Langthorne, M. (2016). *Somebody to Love: The Life, Death and Legacy of Freddie Mercury*. London: Blink Publishing.

Rojek, C. (2001). *Celebrity*. London: Reaktion Books Ltd.

Scawen, S. (1991, April 29). Tragic face of Freddie Mercury. *The Sun*. p. 1.

Smith, R. (2016). *Seduced and Abandoned: Essays on Gay Men and Popular Music*. London, New York: Bloomsbury Academic.

Sutcliffe, P. (2009). *Queen: The Ultimate Illustrated History of the Crown Kings of Rock*. Minneapolis, MN: MBI Publishing Company.

Townsend, M. (1992, February). The Queen is Dead. *Record Hunter* in *Vox*, *17*, 1-5, 10.

Webb, J. (1974, April 4). Just A Regular Kinda Guy. *New Musical Express*. Retrieved from http://www.queenonline.com/en/the-band/interviews/freddie-mercury-1/just-a-regular-kinda-guy/.

Whittow, H. (1986, October 18). Do I Look Like I'm Dying of AIDS? Fumes Freddie. *The Sun*. Retrieved from http://www.queencuttings.com/dblog/stampa.asp?articolo=191.

Paul Newman: Posthumous Philanthropy and Persona

Jackie Raphael

Abstract. Hollywood in the 1950s brought us many iconic stars such as James Dean, Marilyn Monroe, Marlon Brando, Steve McQueen and Paul Newman. Newman is remembered for films such as *Cat on a Hot Tin Roof* (1958), *Cool Hand Luke* (1967) and *Butch Cassidy and the Sundance Kid* (1969). However, he was not just an actor, but also a car racer and a philanthropist. He is known for his long-lasting marriage (50 years to Joanne Woodward) and his charity food-dressing label, which helped reinforce his identity as a nice guy in Hollywood. In comparison to the other actors listed, Newman was not known as a rebel, but as a handsome, cool and kind man. By setting up his philanthrocapitalist-structured foundation, Paul Newman's Own in 1982, he solidified this image. On the labels of the jars his face and name appear, working as a way to introduce him to future generations while also lending his identity to an ongoing charity organization. Another example of his philanthropic legacy is the Hole in the Wall Camp, which he co-founded in 1988, to help sick children. Through focusing on a case study of Paul Newman, it is established that a celebrity can make a difference long-term. However, to have a posthumous brand that keeps on selling, one must become iconic. This chapter applies semiotic analysis to Newman's brand to identify and discuss how celebrities can use their status for good, while also establishing a legacy. Newman's films will certainly live on and hopefully so will his charities.

Keywords: Philanthropy, posthumous, persona, branding, authenticity

Introduction

Celebrities are often perceived as having an unreachable status and glamour. When celebrities attach themselves to a charity or cause, they add a sense of kindness to their brand. Philanthropy can make a celebrity seem humble and somewhat relatable to the public if they share the same views. From a publicity perspective, it is key to building a celebrity's brand. However, the level of involvement certainly varies between celebrities. While some may attend charity events, others are photographed helping people in third-world countries, some become UN ambassadors and some create their own charity organization. However, regardless of the varying levels of involvement, authenticity is the key to successful philanthropy.

This chapter focuses on the philanthropy of actor Paul Newman. Newman is renowned as a kind man, car racer, devoted husband (50 years to Joanne Woodward) and talented actor. He is most recognized for his roles in *Cat on a Hot Tin Roof* (1958), *Cool Hand Luke* (1967) and *Butch Cassidy and the*

Sundance Kid (1969). Newman created two key charities, which have lived on post-death. The first is Paul Newman's Own in 1982 and the second is the Hole in the Wall Camp, which he co-founded in 1988, to help sick children. Through these organizations, Newman fought for social change and supported those in need. This chapter applies semiotic analysis and McCracken's meaning transfer theory to Newman's brand to analyze how he built his image and what legacy he has left behind. As a result, this exploration opens the discussion about how an icon's brand can impact contemporary social issues and how modern day celebrities can learn from this and establish a similar brand strategy for themselves long-term.

Celebrity Philanthropy

To understand the way in which celebrity philanthropy works, one must first define these two key terms. Philanthropy is defined in the simplest way as; "The desire to promote the welfare of others, expressed especially by the generous donation of money to good causes" (Oxford Dictionaries, 2016). However, Thorup (2013) breaks down the various ideological approaches to philanthropy:

> Consumer philanthropy, in which we are asked to consume with good conscience; corporate philanthropy, in which businesses engage in social work and philanthropic associations reengineer themselves to mimic corporations; billionaire philanthropy, in which conspicuous consumption is now being supplemented with conspicuous philanthropy; and celebrity philanthropy, in which one of the hallmarks of being a celebrity today consists in the commitment to turn that fame towards a good purpose. (p. 555)

Thorup summarizes these categories under the term 'philanthrocapitalism', which is defined as the combination of capitalism and charity. This paper focuses predominantly on 'celebrity philanthropy', through the lens of a case study of Paul Newman. As a result, 'consumer philanthropy' is additionally explored in looking at the Newman's Own foundation, which takes some inspiration from the corporate philanthropic approach. In this case, those who purchase the product may be charitable consumers and/or dedicated Newman fans.

In discussing 'celebrity philanthropy', Thorup (2013) stated; "we find philanthropy offering itself as a way to deal with the problem of legitimate inequality" (p. 569). He is referring to the inequality in the way celebrities live their lives versus the way the general public lives. This of course varies depending on the level of celebrity or who one considers a celebrity.

As Jeffreys and Allatson (2015) explained some celebrities are objects of "worship" as they are known for their talents, while others are considered notorious, as their fame is the result of "media exposure" (p. 6). Similarly, Chris Rojek (2001) identified three categories of fame – ascribed, achieved and attributed. Acknowledging these definitions, Paul Newman is classified as having 'achieved' celebrity status, as he was 'worshiped' by his fans and the media for the work he created. Rojek (2001) defined achieved status as those who "are recognized as individuals who possess rare talents or skills" (p.18). Newman's acting career established his fame and led him to his iconic status. Icons must "embody qualities that their fans want to emulate and their appeal is timeless, crossing continents and spanning generations" (Millidge & Hodge, 2010, p. 6). There are varying levels of iconic status, just as there are varying levels of fame. While Newman may not be as iconic as Elvis Presley, his status still holds great value.

As a celebrity, Newman is also considered a brand. Banet-Weiser (2012) stated; "a brand is the perception – the series of images, themes, morals, values, feelings, and sense of authenticity conjured by the product itself" (p. 4). While Banet-Weiser focuses on a product's branding, her discussion of branding and authenticity is also relevant to a celebrity's image. A person's 'brand identity' is the way consumers view them. The celebrity is the 'brand' and the public portrayal of their lifestyle and personality is the 'identity'. They can then use this brand to sell other brands through the meaning transfer process.

Grant McCracken's (1989) meaning transfer process was based on the way in which a celebrity's endorsement of a product or service transfers the celebrity's identity to the brand and then on to the final consumer. For example, if the celebrity represents the essence of 'cool', that then makes the product appear cool and the user feels the same way when utilizing the product. Many researchers have applied McCracken's model, including Tripp, Jensen and Carlson (1994, p. 535), Erdogan (2000), Dorn (2001), Harris (2002, p. 30) and Choi and Rifon (2007). McCracken's theories are also applicable in examining philanthropy. A celebrity's identity is shared with the charity, which then makes those who donate feel some connection to that celebrity. This theory is applied in the Newman case study to demonstrate the significance of his attachment to the charities. Barthes' theories on semiotics are further applied to break down the visual representation of Newman's Own and how it sells.

As explained by Keel and Nataraajan; "Celebrities have long been used to sell products, dating back to the second half of the nineteenth century" (2012, p. 690). The endorsement industry has expanded greatly since then with 17 percent of advertisements featuring celebrities in the 1970s and 25 percent by 2003 (Keel & Nataraajan 2012). The dependence on celebrities in advertising is evident through the large sums of money companies are willing to pay for their brand association. For example, golfer Tiger Woods reportedly earned over $23 million annually for his endorsements prior to his brand being tarnished by his infidelity (2012, p. 690). Many of Woods' contracts were long-spanning, indicating the companies felt that the investment was worth continuing. Newman had been in the celebrity industry for many decades and was aware of the value of celebrity status. Thus, Newman chose to use his own identity to sell a product, but rather than gaining the profit, he gave it to charity, which further enhanced his image as a kind man.

As Keel and Nataraajan stated:

> Despite the increase in celebrity branding and endorsements, it seems that many celebrities' attempts to extend their brands have not fared well. Several celebrity restaurants have closed: Dive! closed in May 1999; Schwarzenegger sold Schatzi's in 1998, and it closed soon after; Jennifer Lopez's Latin restaurant, Madre's, closed in 2008. Celebrity fashion lines have also experienced turmoil: Jennifer Lopez's sportswear brand Sweetface has been in hiatus since 2009, recording artists Eminem's and Eve's fashion lines burned out quickly, and Snoop Dogg's clothing line was discontinued in 2003 after three years (Agins, 2005). (p. 694)

The reason for these failures can vary from financial investments, branding strategies, the celebrity's own career success and much more. In the case of Newman's Own, Newman's iconic status helps to support the company's brand. The charitable aspect of the brand also helps to entice consumers. Another key aspect of his charity organizations is authenticity.

Photographs of Newman actively participating and interacting with children at the Hole in the Wall Camp and the story of how he created the first salad dressing for Newman's Own adds a sense of authenticity to these foundations, as will be discussed later in the chapter. Authenticity is all about perception and believability. Having a well-known and likable face attached to a brand can help to gain attention and some sense of trust. If something appears to be credible, it is more likely to be consumed or donated to. While the public can never know Newman's 'true' intentions when creating his charities, they can choose to accept the story that is told to them through his media presence. Regardless, they must first perceive him as authentic. Thus, the formation of his brand identity was crucial to the success of his foundations, as the organizations are reliant on his celebrity image.

Newman's Own Brand Identity

Paul Newman was born on January 26, 1925 in Ohio, United States of America and died on September 26, 2008 (Paul Newman's Own, 2016). In 83 years,

Newman starred in 76 films and was nominated for an Academy Award 10 times, which he eventually won for *The Color of Money* in 1986 (2016). Other successful films include *Cat on a Hot Tin Roof* (1958), *Cool Hand Luke* (1967) and *Butch Cassidy* and *the Sundance Kid* (1969). Newman is renowned not only for his acting talent, but also his car racing skills, his bright blue eyes, his charitable nature, his close friendship with Robert Redford and his 50 years of marriage to actress Joanne Woodward. One of Newman's most famous quotes is in reference to his wife; "I have steak at home, why go out for hamburgers?" (100lizi, 2009). Newman and Woodward appeared in 11 films together, and are the only Hollywood couple to both win Academy Awards while still being married to one another (Paul Newman's Own, 2016). This is one of the many reasons their lasting marriage seems to be fascinating to the media. Three years after making a film with Woodward about car racing, Newman decided to start racing (100lizi, 2009). It was 1972 and he was 47 years old (2009). He continued to race into his 80s, winning many national championships (2009). These facts are what contribute to Newman's brand identity as a caring, cool and charismatic man.

Throughout his career, Newman was attached to various endorsements including Maxwell, Coke, Datsun, Canon, Skyline, Nissan, Rolex, McDonalds, PacifiCare, Lux and Fuji Card. The last two were overseas campaigns, showing his global status. Lux in particular focused on his blue eyes in the advertisement. However, the remaining companies listed were related to sponsorship of his racing. Perhaps the most personalized of all the endorsements, was the advertisement for Rolex. In the advert, a voice-over explains that Newman's wife had given him a Rolex Daytona and engraved it with the message "drive slowly" (Kovats, 2013). The backstory adds a sense of authenticity to the endorsement and is supported by visuals of Newman wearing the watch.

By attaching their brands to Newman, the meaning transferred to these companies was that they too were classy, sexy and adventurous. Although Newman's racing hobby came later in life, his brand essence remained. Similarly, by gaining sponsorship by such large companies, Newman's racing status grew. However, the strongest brand association that Newman left behind was the foundation, Newman's Own.

Newman's Philanthropy

What began as a simple gift to family and friends became an international foundation that has raised more than $460 million in 34 years (Newman's Own Foundation, 2016). Paul Newman had created a salad dressing that he decided to sell under the brand Newman's Own and in the first year it made a profit of

$300,000 (2016). Newman decided to give this profit to charity and then in the following years expanded his product range to include pasta sauces, lemonade, popcorn and salsa (2016). "In 2005, Paul established Newman's Own Foundation to ensure that the company's philanthropic outreach would continue" (2016). After Newman's death, the company expanded their range further to include frozen pizza and skillet meals, reaching more than 100 products (2016). Ultimately, Newman used his celebrity status to create a philanthrocapitalist approach to his foundation that continued after his death.

Newman also used his fame to create The Hole in the Wall Gang Camp, which began in 1988 and expanded in 2012 to reach children globally, becoming known as SeriousFun Children's Network. While the original camp still exists in Connecticut, the umbrella organization includes 29 other camps including Camp Korey, Camp Colors of Love, Camp Hope, Camp Rainbow and Over the Wall (SeriousFun Children's Network, 2016). All of these camps continue the work that Newman began with the goal of making sick children feel like they are not in a hospital environment and allowing them the opportunity to enjoy life.

The original name of the camp came from a reference to his film *Butch Cassidy and the Sundance Kid*. The charity still refers to Newman as the founder and shares his story, maintaining his philanthropic brand. However, it is the Newman's Own brand strategy that he is mostly recognized for within his philanthropy. The products themselves not only bear his name, but also have his face on the labels. The main company logo is an illustration of Newman smiling in a chef's uniform. His image is adjusted thematically to reflect the product being sold. For example, a Mexican styled salsa shows Newman with a large moustache, while an Italian pasta sauce shows him wearing an old style flat cap. On a connotative level, these images not only reflect the theme of the product, but also create a fun tone of voice for the company. This represents Newman's cheeky personality and the light-hearted approach to this charity organization.

The organic range was launched by his daughter, Nell Newman, and shows the two of them in a parody of the American Gothic painting by Grant Wood. This continues the humorous tone of voice. The image allowed for the brand to introduce Newman's daughter, but still included his face to reinforce the authenticity between the two subsections of the company. Authenticity was first established in that Newman spoke about making the products himself, especially the original salad dressing. The company is also upfront in informing consumers of which products were actually originally made by Newman, his daughter or other people in the organization. This allows for the foundation to maintain its credibility and the trust of their audience.

The original labels also included copywriting by Paul Newman, who stated in an interview with Jay Leno that he writes them himself (100lizi, 2009). The labels reinforce the tone of voice, as can be read in this example from a jar:

> Working twelve hour days… wrecked… hungry… arrive home, deserted by wife and children…cursing! Scan the cupboard – one package spaghetti…one bottle pasta sauce…run to the kitchen, cook – junk! YUK! Lie down, snooze…visions of culinary delights…Venetian ancestor tickles my ear, tickle, tickle…sauce talk…MAMA MIA! Dash to the vegetable patch… Yum yum…boil water…activate spaghetti…ditto the sauce…slurp, slurp…Terrifico! Magnifico! Slurp! Caramba! Bottle the sauce!... share with guys on street car… ah, me, finally immortal!

This tone has continued in the products made by the organization after Newman's death. The consistency in the branding allowed for the company to establish itself, while the variety in the labelling is playful and encourages people to collect the range. For committed fans, collecting these labels would be enjoyable. For casual consumers, it would allow for new products to standout on the shelves. The overall concept that a consumer can donate money by purchasing this product over its competitors also allows for the public to feel good about their purchasing decision. This philanthrocapitalism can encourage brand loyalty and ongoing charity payments. The foundation also localizes the charitable branding by stating on their website and on the products how much money has been donated to their country. This adds a sense of national pride for the consumer.

As Thorup (2013) explained, there is a growing need for consumers to feel good about their purchasing choices; "This moral surplus value is embedded in the shopping situation itself, at the heart of the basic market relation of buying and selling" (p. 560). However, Newman began doing this long before the trend was particularly strong. This originality is what contributes to his brand identity.

Overall, by placing Newman's name and face on the products, the meaning transfer process allows for the company to represent a sense of being fun, charitable and original. The end consumer then feels a sense of doing good, while also being entertained by the labels and brand. For dedicated fans they may also feel some connection to Newman. The way in which Newman set up the foundation has allowed it to continue to grow in the eight years since his death. It is likely to continue for years to come, which also means his visual identity will continue to be a reminder of his success both in his film career and his philanthropy. However, it is threatened by the management of the foundation, which was left in the hands of Robert H. Forrester. A *Vanity Fair* article by Mark Seal from 2015 outlines the details of the disagreement between

Newman's family and Forrest, in relation to finances and control of Newman's Own. Seal (2015) suggests in the article that perhaps Newman's memory had been fading in the final months of his life due to his illness. Seal (2015) reports that Newman had adjusted his will repeatedly in the final year and the last version was completed six months before his death.

One particular point made in this article is that the Scott Newman Center, which Newman had created in 1980, after the loss of his son, was no longer funded by Newman's Own (Seal, 2015). As a result, it closed in May 2013 (2015). This seems misaligned with Newman's persona, although Forrester claims they had discussed this decision prior to his death. Nell Newman is quoted with various other arguments suggesting that Forrester is not fulfilling her father's legacy, as he would have wanted (2015). While it is not the focus of this chapter to decipher who is right or wrong in this battle of finances and control, it does raise concerns of how Newman's Own will continue to celebrate Newman's legacy and represent his brand posthumously. Ultimately, in the eight years since his death, his brand identity has continued to be represented as a philanthropic star.

Leaving a Legacy

In the year of his death, Forbes reported that Newman's Own had earned $120 million in the previous year and that "the residuals from a lifetime of high-profile movie roles" came to five million dollars (Hoy, 2008). Thus, even at the age of 83, his income was high due to the many successful films he had created throughout his life and his charity organization was continuing to succeed. Newman's philanthropy has inspired many others to do the same. For example, actor Hugh Jackman spoke about creating his coffee brand on *The Weekly* in 2015; "I was really inspired by Paul Newman and what he did with Paul Newman's Own. I thought, well I'm going to do the same. Not a big fan of salad dressing. Big fan of coffee" (2015).

Many other celebrities have also spoken about Newman fondly, focusing more on his philanthropy than his acting. Actor Paul Rudd commented on his giving nature:

> You know who's a good role model? Paul Newman. I just think he's an example of somebody who came into this world, and left this world, as a contributor in ways that are so huge. Even though the world has a lot of problems in it, it is better off by a mile for Paul Newman having lived in it. He gave more than he got. He got a lot, but he gave way, way more. (Wilson, 2008)

Leonardo DiCaprio was asked about Newman after his death and also referred to him as a role model in both his acting and philanthropy:

> He was the great role model for anyone in this industry, in the [way] that he conducted his life. Look at him, and look at the man's work. As an actor, he was part of the definitive group of actors who really shaped what modern acting is. Yet, at the same time, he was a normal family man, and extremely philanthropic. His foundation will continue to do great things for children all around the world. He is really the role model; he's what you want to aspire to be in this industry, both professionally and personally. (Carroll, 2008)

These are just some of the many quotes from celebrities that admired Newman. Whether they knew him or not he left an impression on the industry and inspired others to be philanthropic. "Renowned for being close friends, Robert Redford stated after Newman's death; 'There is a point where feelings go beyond words. I have lost a real friend. My life — and this country — is better for his being in it'" (Carroll, 2008). In an interview with Leno just a few years before he passed away, Newman said he and Redford were working on a few projects together (100lizi, 2009). Ultimately, their friendship had continued for many decades and Newman's desire to keep working in his 80s also represented his persona. He reflected a resilient work ethic and a passion for both his film career and philanthropy.

Newman left behind a strong legacy, which is being maintained by various people. However, it is often the other celebrities in the industry who can help a brand to live on. Jake Gyllanhaal was Newman's godson and attended the SeriousFun event in his honor in 2012. He spoke about Newman fondly for his philanthropy rather than his acting, which was the focus of the event (In Touch Weekly, 2012). By having his presence at such an occasion, it also helped to draw attention to the charity and introduce a new generation of fans to Newman. Similarly, in 2015 George Clooney, Meryl Streep and Tom Hanks presented at the event. This can help Newman's brand live on and his charities to continue by reaching other clusters of fans.

Another example of his memory being honored is the 2015 ceremony held in Newman's hometown to release a postal Forever Stamp (United States Postal Service, 2015). It refers to him as both an actor and philanthropist. It is gestures such as this and the annual SeriousFun events that help to maintain Newman's brand identity and recognize the work he achieved by not just lending his name, but creating foundations that actively make a difference.

Conclusion

Newman is among many other 'cool' 1950s celebrities whose career lasted longer than most. However, his legacy is built upon his enduring marriage and his charitable identity. These are elements of his brand that standout against others. He solidified this image through his Newman's Own product range. For a celebrity to follow in Newman's footsteps, they need to first establish a successful career and strong brand identity. They then need to create a charity that bear more than just their name but also their visual identity. While many celebrities create product ranges such as perfumes, bags and clothing lines, these do not secure them as icons. In a world where many products are either 'created' by celebrities or endorsed by them, it is unlikely to establish the identity of a celebrity long-term. Iconic status is reliant on many aspects of a celebrity. Their work must stand the test of time, their persona must be liked by the masses and their brand must standout against their competitors.

Creating a foundation in one's name is not enough. It is the visual identity that helps an icon be established. It is also the control of that identity that is important. Companies such as CMG Worldwide maintain celebrity brands including James Dean and Marilyn Monroe, controlling how their image is used. However, it seems a large portion of Newman's brand is currently in the hands of Forrester. Yet, after he eventually passes, it is unknown who will maintain Newman's Own brand and what will be done with it.

Further research is needed in looking at the current perception of Newman's brand identity to examine the longevity of his status. Exploration of other celebrities who have created charities that have been maintained posthumously can also help to draw comparisons and gain a stronger understanding of how a celebrity's brand can live on and philanthropy can be long-lasting. The world needs more philanthrocapitalism approaches, as it helps to create a long-term strategy. The celebrity brand is enhanced, the fans/consumers feel happy with their purchasing choices and the charities benefit. As Thorup (2013) explained; "You get the product and its utility value but you also get to do some good" (p. 560). Further research should be done in creating a sustainable foundation that allows for this system.

There is only so much one can do to maintain their brand after death. Newman certainly did his best to set up a lasting brand, although it is possibly under threat. Regardless, his persona as a compassionate and generous man remains. Ultimately, an authentic brand and philanthropy can lead to an enduring identity and an ongoing charity organization. Iconic status is difficult to establish but also holds a lot of capital in the world of consumption. Newman set up his legacy, however the threats Newman's Own faces could impact his posthumous brand.

References

100lizi. (2009). *Paul Newman and Joanne Woodward on their marriage.* Retrieved from https://www.youtube.com/watch?v=hMLMWpSHdZE.

100lizi. (2009). *Paul Newman with Jay Leno 08-04-2005 part 1/2.* Retrieved from https://www.youtube.com/watch?v=-xsYRKunZpk.

Banet-Weiser, S. (2012). *AuthenticTM: The Politics of Ambivalence in a Brand Culture,* New York: New York University Press.

Carroll, L. (2008). Stars Remember Paul Newman: 'He's what you aspire to be,' Leonardo DiCaprio says. *MTV News.* Retrieved from http://www.mtv.com/news/1595822/stars-remember-paul-newman-hes-what-you-aspire-to-be-leonardo-dicaprio-says/.

Choi, S. M., & Rifon, N. J. (2007). Who is the Celebrity in Advertising? Understanding Dimensions of Celebrity Images. *The Journal of Popular Culture, 40*(2), 304-324. http://dx.doi.org/10.1111/j.1540-5931.2007.00380.x.

Dorn, J. G. v. (2001). *Constructed Communities: The First Decade of Nike Women's Advertising.* (PhD diss.). The University of Wisconsin, Madison. Retrieved from www.proquest.com.

Erdogan, B. Z. (2000). *Constructing a Practitioner-Based Model of Selecting Celebrity Endorsers.* Doctor of Philosophy (PhD diss.). The University of Strathclyde, Glasgow. Retrieved from http://ethos.bl.uk.

Harris, F. J. (2002). *Internal Factors Affecting Brand Performance.* (PhD diss.). The Open University, United Kingdom. Retrieved from http://oro.open.ac.uk/19913/.

Hoy, P. (2008). Top-Earning Dead Celebrities. *Forbes.* Retrieved from http://www.forbes.com/2008/10/27/top-dead-celebrity-biz-media-deadcelebs08-cz_ph_1027celeb.html.

In Touch Weekly. (2012). *Jake Gyllenhaal Talks To In Touch At "A Celebration Of Paul Newman's Dream" In NYC.* Retrieved from https://www.youtube.com/watch?v=8uAXlpjQDRM.

Jeffreys, E., & Allatson, P. (2015). *Celebrity Philanthropy.* Bristol, UK: Intellect.

Keel, A., & Nataraajan, R. (2012). Celebrity Endorsements and Beyond: New Avenues for Celebrity Branding. *Psychology and Marketing, 29*(9): 690–703. doi: 10.1002/mar.20555.

Kovats, T. (2013). *Rolex Paul Newman Daytona Commercial 2013.* Retrieved from https://www.youtube.com/watch?v=_Kz_40Tac3U.

Millidge, J., & Hodge, J. (2010). *Icons.* Sywell: Igloo.

Newman's Own Foundation. (2016). *History*. Retrieved from http://newmansownfoundation.org/about-us/history/.

Oxford Dictionaries. (2016). *Philanthropy*. Retrieved from http://www.oxforddictionaries.com/definition/english/philanthropy.

Paul Newman's Own. (2016). *Paul Fast Facts*. Retrieved from http://www.paulnewmansown.com.au/our-story/pauls-fast-facts.html.

Rojek, C. (2001). *Celebrity*. London: Reaktion Books.

Seal, M. (2015). Inside the family battle for the Newman's Owen brand name. *Vanity Fair HIVE*. Retrieved from http://www.vanityfair.com/news/2015/07/paul-newmans-own-family-feud-susan-newman.

SeriousFun Children's Network. (2016). *Find a Camp*. Retrieved from http://www.seriousfunnetwork.org/camps-and-programs/find-a-camp.

The Weekly. (2015). *The Weekly: Hugh Jackman extended interview*. Retrieved from https://www.youtube.com/watch?v=fJWawKeXOEk.

Thorup, M. (2013). Pro bono? on philanthrocapitalism as ideological answer to inequality. *Ephemera, 13*(3), 555-576. Retrieved from http://search.proquest.com.dbgw.lis.curtin.edu.au/docview/1465501564?accountid=10382.

Tripp, C., Jensen, T. D., & Carlson, L. (1994). The Effects of Multiple Product Endorsements by Celebrities on Consumers' Attitudes and Intentions, *Journal of Consumer Research, 20*(4), 535-547. Retrieved from http://www.jstor.org/stable/2489757.

United States Postal Service. (2015). *Paul Newman Forever Stamp on Sale Today*. Retrieved from https://about.usps.com/news/national-releases/2015/pr15_052.htm.

Wilson, J. (2008). Paul Rudd, 'Role Model'? He doesn't think so. *CNN*. Retrieved from http://edition.cnn.com/2008/SHOWBIZ/Movies/10/29/paul.rudd/index.html?eref=rss_latest.

www.ingramcontent.com/pod-product-compliance
Lightning Source LLC
Chambersburg PA
CBHW050654270326
41927CB00012B/3019